Mike .

Best wishes

Raman Shroe Finn

Now that Geoff Boycott
has been rejected you and
I can open for Yorkshire!

R x.

HEYHOE!

HEYHOE!

The autobiography of
Rachael Heyhoe Flint

Foreword by Eric Morecambe

PELHAM BOOKS

LONDON

First published in Great Britain by
PELHAM BOOKS LTD
52 Bedford Square
London WC1B 3EF
1978

ISBN 0 7207 1049 9

Printed in Great Britain by Tonbridge Printers Ltd, Kent
and bound by Redwood Burn, Esher, Surrey

Contents

Acknowledgement

The author is grateful to Alan Lee for his help in compiling this book.

Illustrations

Acknowledgements for Illustrations
The author and publisher would like to express their
thanks to the following for permission to reproduce
the photographs: Michael Alcott (33), Daniel Allmark
Photography (19), Apex Photos Ltd (7), Associated
Newspapers Group Ltd (17), *Birmingham Post and
Mail* (23), Martin Clement (12 – photographer Harvey
Bilt), Central Press (4), *Daily Express* (18), *Evening
Standard* (24), *Herald and Weekly Times,* Melbourne
(10), Maurice Jones (6), Ken Kelly (32, 34, 35),
Keystone Press Agency (21 – photographer Chris
Ware, 29 – photographer Ian Tyas), Morley L. Pecker
(20), Press Association Ltd (27), Tate & Lyle
(Refineries) Ltd (15), Wey Studio (30)
Thanks are also due to the following for permission to
reproduce the cartoons: Giles and the *Sunday
Express* (pages 21 and 43), *The Herald and Weekly
Times,* Melbourne (page 76), Trog and the *Observer*
(page 158), Roy Ullyett (page 99)

Foreword

When I first heard the name Rachael Heyhoe Flint I thought it was a singing group. Well, you can't win 'em all. I remember when I mentioned Showaddywaddy to Ernie Wise he went into an Indian restaurant and ordered it.

But through the years, I began to hear more of Rachael when, as Rachael Heyhoe, she became Britain's best-known woman cricketer, thus striking a formidable blow for Women's Liberation. Over the years, Rachael has got more on the scoreboard than there have been runs on the pound!

It would be easy for me to pepper this foreword with such witticisms as bowling the maidens over, a miss with a hit, caught in her slips or getting into trouble with a Chinaman. However, I will leave such chores to my play-writing partner who understands cricket far more than me. I know that when he first heard the hit tune 'Amazing Grace' he said it was about time that we paid a tribute to the great W.G.!

What do you think of it so far? You do? Well read on. Rachael first worked on a Wolverhampton newspaper, combining her journalistic duties with international cricket and hockey. She married Mr Flint (a hard man!) and so became Rachael Heyhoe Flint thus carrying the initials R.H.F. You might think that the poor fellow would object, but not he. When asked what R.H.F. stands for he always says 'ruddy handsome fellow', or 'right-hand Fred'.

Since those early days in Wolverhampton A.B.W. (After Billy Wright), Rachael has added to her many talents as a speaker, a radio and TV personality and as an author. She is one of our best after-dinner speakers and she is in such demand that she rarely eats at home. In fact, her lonely husband has eaten so many frozen dinners that he's been treated for a chilblained stomach and has had a gas heater fitted in his igloo. And Rachael has eaten chicken dinners to such an extent that she's been banned by the RSPCA!

Of course, Rachael has learnt a few tricks. She now carries an extra large handbag with a refrigerated interior. This means that she can easily transfer meat and poultry into it while a dinner is in progress. And although she might feel hungry by the time the dinner is over, Rachael now has the best cold meat store in Petticoat Lane. Which, you must admit, is a neat way to get to 'Petticoat Line', one of the many radio programmes that used the talents of Rachael. She's equally at home on 'Any Questions?' In fact Rachael is here, there and everywhere; just like the elusive pimple. Don't worry; with her personality she's not going to be squeezed out!

But seriously, readers. I'm very happy to be writing about a great sportswoman and a unique personality. Rachael Heyhoe Flint, MBE, has a lot to say in this book and, I hope, in many other books to come.

Eric Morecambe, OBE

Preface

I have in my possession a coat of arms supposedly attributed to the Heyhoe family, and the Latin motto *Amor et Amicitia* inscribed underneath the shield means 'Love and Friendship'.

I think my life in sport has been one of love and friendship and I like to think of the words of a great supporter of women's cricket, the third duke of Dorset who wrote in 1777 in the *Ladies & Gentlemen's Magazine*: 'What is human life but a game of cricket? And if so why should not the ladies play it as well as we?'

When I was asked to 'do' my autobiography my initial reaction was that I hadn't finished yet! Once you become involved in the friendly and exciting world of sport, media and promotion you step on to a roundabout almost as magic as the one belonging to Dougal, Florence, Zebbedee and Brian the Snail.

So who knows what the future holds? Obviously I cannot be a Peter Pan of sport and continue playing cricket and hockey until I qualify for the Geriatrics XI but I would like to hope that I can put back into sport just a little of the enjoyment that it has given me.

With a deep-seated interest in politics – albeit rather peripheral at the moment – I could dream that I might one day become minister of sport. I could then be a sort of Robin Hood and rob the very rich in sport to give to their poor companions. I have long felt that there is a tremendous imbalance in the distribution of wealth in this area: for example, a professional footballer can make a cool five per cent of a £400,000 transfer fee – namely £20,000 – merely by moving from one club to another, provided he didn't *ask* to be transferred. For that amount of money I wouldn't mind moving from Wolverhampton to Hartlepool!

I mentioned that I wanted to be a blue female version of Denis Howell (blue in political terms not in language!) to Margaret Thatcher at a reception in London shortly after she had become leader of the Conservative Party. I hope she hasn't forgotten the comment she made to me when she knew of my ambition: 'I'll bear that in mind!'

Taking on such a role would certainly mean challenging male supremacy, but I've been doing that for years anyway so it wouldn't be anything different! By that token it doesn't mean that I'm Women's Lib. – far from it, because I value that bit of underwear they rush out and burn each week with a matinee on Wednesdays. I, too, believe in good support.

Speaking of challenging men brings to mind the dozens of occasions when I have taken a women's cricket XI to face various showbiz, club and even county sides all over the country. We really found trouble when in one match in Hertfordshire we dismissed the club 'big-head' first ball – much to the amusement of his jeering friends who had left the bar for the only moment of the day to witness his downfall. But that was where we made the mistake, because that deflated fellow came on to bowl later in the match. Normally, I gather, he took only a short run up, but in order to vent his male aggression on me (I was batting at the time) he marked his run out until he was just about visible on the distant boundary, stood there pawing the ground like a rampant bull and then hurtled towards me like an Apollo mission space-launch from Cape Kennedy! That is when the moment of truth arrives and you realise that there are ways and ways of trying to compete with the 'stronger sex'. (That should win me a few supporters!)

So my feelings are that if I display enough Heyhoe-type love and friendship there are still many more things which 'I have left undone, which I ought to have done', which in turn will keep me on that magic roundabout.

A few years ago, when I appeared on Pete Murray's 'Open House' programme on Radio 2, a graphologist (who had never met me) analysed my handwriting. Having read his judgement, you may then pass forward to the rest of the book and decide whether Heyhoe really is the sort of person he described. Having re-read that same judgement, I have decided that I must go out and change my writing!

It is the handwriting of a person with a determined nature. Basically she is calm, placid and friendly – but she does like to get her own way.

The embellished but quite dominant 'I' shows her determination, willpower and self-confidence. She dislikes fuss and is able to get down to essentials.

She is not the type to put on airs and graces and is likely instinctively to dislike people who do . . . she has the ability to take the mickey out of such people.

The formation of the writing and quite frequent breaks shout of creative ability. I feel sure this creative ability is put to some constructive and practical purpose. If it is in the painting sphere she is more likely to paint the house than canvas. If it is in the writing sphere it is likely to be directed towards a non-fiction subject rather than a romantic novel.

The flashing connections between the 'w' and 'h' combined with the dots show her fiery spirit and instant wit. It makes me wonder if she has ever gone in for humorous writing. Certainly she is a good story-teller with a good store of anecdotes.

I promise you I didn't invent a word of that, and that the graphologist who compiled the data had never seen me in his life – the lucky fellow!

As the analysis states, I hate fuss, but only of a certain sort. I have loved some of the fuss which certain men's cricket clubs have extended towards us – particularly the one in Auckland, New Zealand, where we had to use the men's changing-rooms and facilities during our match. The ground authorities there felt that we might be embarrassed gazing at the marble walls in the men's loos so to spare our feminine blushes, they had arranged a most immaculate display of exotic colourful hot-house plants to cover the troughs!

It is not in my nature to rumble and grumble, but I hope you will forgive me if a few recent incidents have temporarily altered my outlook on life. 'Do not adjust your sets: the interference is purely temporary – there is a fault.'

I always remember how, on my school report, our music mistress wrote: 'Rachael has obvious musical talent but I do wish she would not produce her voice in such a harsh manner.' (I used to like to sing an octave below all the others in the class in a sort of *basso profundo* rendering of 'Nymphs and Shepherds'!)

I trust that I have not 'produced my voice' in too harsh a manner in this book and that by the time you have ploughed through it you will feel the 'Love and Friendship' which I have experienced throughout my days as 'Batwoman'.

1 Run Out

My eleven-year reign as England captain ended abruptly on a Sunday afternoon in mid-July 1977. Fittingly, the sun didn't shine that day: it was damp, dark and drizzling, and as I walked across the cricket pitch in Halifax it seemed as if I was walking to the gallows; my stomach felt empty and I was strangely nervous.

The concluding trial match of the 1977 season, designed to finalise the selectors' plans for the forthcoming World Cup series in India, had been abandoned because of the rain, and now a message had been sent, summoning me across the ground to meet the selectors in the nearby tennis pavilion. Logically, I should have had no cause to fear. The previous summer's tour by Australia had been a success in every way and my personal form had seemed reasonable, with an average of 87.5 and my career best, 179. I had been captain of my country for eleven years, during which we had not suffered a single Test match defeat.

But deep down, I knew exactly what to expect. In the past, being re-named as captain had only entailed my being taken aside for a brief moment in the dressing-room prior to an official announcement – never anything so formal as a meeting with the selectors. Something, I knew instinctively, was wrong, and the sinking feeling in the pit of my stomach told me that this was to be the *coup de grâce* at the end of twelve months in which the rapport which had always previously existed between the Women's Cricket Association and myself had visibly begun to crumble.

I remember that hundred-yard stroll so vividly, from leaving my friends in the hubbub of the dressing-room, through being vaguely aware of mist clinging to the hills away to my left and an appalling smell wafting up from the nearby canal, to the moment when I arrived beneath the tennis pavilion balcony, face-to-face with four suitably solemn expressions ...

Audrey Winterbottom, chairman of the selectors, was leaning poker-faced over the balcony, and even at such a serious moment in my life I pictured her as a sea-sick traveller about to cast herself overboard. Kay Green, Sue Hilliam and Carole Evans, three of the other four selectors, sat silently apart. They looked blankly ahead as though they had been hypnotised! Audrey Disbury, the fifth selector, was not at that final match – I wondered if her absence was significant, for she had always been a very good friend of mine. Like the prisoner in the dock, I waited for sentence to be passed.

It seemed somehow intended that I should be standing at ground level, with the rain steadily soaking my unprotected head as I looked up at the chairman. Our opening exchange was ridiculously trite. 'Thank you for coming,' she said. 'It's a pleasure,' I replied.

Then Audrey Winterbottom drew breath, but still she couldn't bring herself to look me in the eye. Instead, staring vacantly over my head, she stiffly announced: 'I think I ought to tell you that you are not going to be named as captain for the touring team to India in December.'

However well one is prepared for any shock, it is never very easy to grasp when it actually happens, although in my mind I had rehearsed this part of the drama. I tried to be phlegmatic about it all, told myself 'that's it, it's over' and prepared to turn and walk away without a word – thinking Shakesperian thoughts like 'Now is the Winterbottom of our discontent' ...! Then I stopped and pulled myself together. After eleven years, I thought, at least I could ask for an explanation. I turned back to Audrey Winterbottom and politely asked: 'Can you tell me why?'

'It's a committee decision,' she replied formally.

'Is it anything to do with my playing form?' I ventured, knowing that logically it couldn't be.

'No.'

'In that case, is it anything I've done off the field?'

'I can't be specific. I cannot point to "A" or "B". It's a committee decision.'

And with that devastatingly frigid closing comment, the interview was obviously over. I saw no point in prolonging it, so muttered an absurd 'thank you' and turned for a walk back that seemed many times longer and more sad than any I had ever made after a dismissal in a match. My thoughts were racing – remember that stiff upper lip I said to myself!

My return was watched by all the players, many of whom had been personal friends over a number of years. They too, had known that all was not well, and as they stood peering through the rain I almost felt an urge to shout to them. Instead I extended one arm out towards them and turned my thumb downwards.

Inside the pavilion a stunned silence reigned – but very different from the one which I had just left, a hundred yards away. I was greeted by expressions of shock and disbelief. Two of the younger girls burst into tears as I shook my head and announced, rather superfluously: 'Sorry, I'm not captain.'

Telling myself I must not break down, I walked on into the dressing-room and began packing my cricket bag. I didn't dare look at anyone, but throughout the packing operation, different girls came up, tapping me on the back, telling me they were sorry and asking what they could do. Of course, the answer was nothing.

I then had a strong urge to go while I could. But I applied all the willpower I could muster and refused to run away before Rosemary Goodchild, the WCA chairman, arrived to make a formal announcement that Mary Pilling was to be the new captain of England. While I stared intently at the ground, an air of shock persisted around the dressing-room, for this had merely added to the insult.

I have nothing whatever against Mary Pilling as a person: we have been team companions and friends for years. But the fact remains that she had been unable to hold her place against Australia the previous summer and possibly might not even have been chosen for the World Cup tour if two of our front-line bowlers had not been forced out of contention by financial difficulties.

In a newspaper interview during the week which followed, Rosemary Goodchild told John Morgan of the *Daily Express* that Mary Pilling had become unavailable for the rest of that Australia series after the first Test due to an injury. This was an utter untruth – she had been dropped because she was not bowling well enough to keep her place.

It wasn't so much her playing ability that made Mary such a strange choice as successor, though. It was her age and complete lack of experience of captaincy which made it almost laughable. I could have understood them appointing a younger captain. If the change-over had been properly handled, I might even have applauded them for their foresight. But Mary Pilling is older than I am! What is more, she had had no experience whatever of captaincy until leading a team in a few Cricket Week festival matches during 1976. Ironically, her side then lost every match!

With all these factors considered, the appointment made less and less sense. It seemed crazy, and very hurtful, and as I collected my kit and packed the car, I still didn't trust myself to speak.

Driving home across the Pennines on the M62, the words 'You are no longer captain of England' rang incessantly in my ears. I could easily have cried. I survived the journey by convincing myself that I had many compensations – a home, a husband and a son, to name just the most important three. When I told Derrick, my husband, what had happened, as he came out to help me unpack the car, he stared at me disbelievingly and said 'That is utterly appalling . . .!'

The story of my sacking made an unimpressive and ambiguous newspaper début in the *Daily Telegraph* the following morning. It was printed as a plain announcement, framed by the WCA, and the inference was clearly that I had either retired or resigned. There was never a chance of it being accepted quite that quietly, however, and I had scarcely managed to get out of bed before things began to move completely out of control.

For the next twelve hours, I seldom escaped from the phone for more than a few minutes at a time. Every reporter's first and obvious question was 'Why'? and I could not give them an adequate answer. I had to tell everyone that I simply hadn't been given a reason, and yet as I took call after call, my mind wandered back to October 1976 and a bizarre meeting in London.

The Australians had just three months previously returned home after a tour that had been promoted and made greater impact than any in the past. That we escaped from defeat by them at the Oval was a minor miracle, for we needed to bat

"Rachael Heyhoe Flint for Captain – that'll make 'em grovel!"

for a day and two thirds and score 245 to avoid an innings defeat. Although I might have been the sheet anchor, the whole team contributed wonderfully; all I told them in the dressing-room before the start of the final day was that I hated losing, that I would do everything in my power to avoid defeat and all I asked for was two-hundred-per-cent support. I got that support – one girl, Jan Allen, batted for an hour for nought; she was in tears when dismissed, but she had played her part.

Ted Hart from the *Manchester Evening News* threw some interesting light on the whole affair with a piece on the Thursday after it had all happened. He was at the Oval and wrote of my eight-and-a-half-hour innings: 'She scored 179 and was finally caught on the boundary rails. As she came into the pavilion a male admirer [my husband] offered her a kiss and a glass of beer. She accepted both readily enough and then beside me I was surprised to hear the voice of dissent: "You would think she's the only player we've got," said a typical committee member. "Wouldn't you just," said her companion, and you could hear the grinding of the knives.'

Also at that Oval match, I was very thrilled to read the words of my hero Colin Cowdrey in *The Cricketer* magazine: 'Thanks to an admirable show of determination by the English batswomen Australia were denied a victory that seemed a foregone conclusion. Rachael Heyhoe Flint's technique and concentration, adopting a role foreign to her temperament, had the look of Sir Leonard Hutton or Geoffrey Boycott at their best. After batting all Tuesday afternoon and throughout the whole of Wednesday, what a pity she did not beat the world record score, as she deserved to do having come so close.'

It is not surprising, therefore, that when I was called down to London to meet the WCA chairman, Rosemary Goodchild (at her request), vice-chairman Mollie Buckland the president, Elspeth Jackson, I assumed it to be no more than an informal review of the summer and general chat over future plans.

My first inkling that this was not the case came with an extraordinary comment from Elspeth Jackson. Having brought me all the way down from Wolverhampton, her opening remark was an unfriendly: 'Let's get down to business, I've got a train to catch.'

She then turned to me and demanded: 'How long do you intend to go on playing cricket?' I replied truthfully that I had considered giving up at the end of the 1976 series, but as I had enjoyed my best-ever year with the bat and could see no logical successor as captain, I hoped I could go on for another year or two.

The interrogation was in full swing now, Rosemary Goodchild stepping in for her turn with a crisp 'How do you see your future with the WCA?'

It all seemed a puzzle to me, but I gave another polite answer, saying that I wanted to continue handling promotions and publicity and generally helping in any way that I could to project the women's game.

Mollie Buckland then gave me the first veiled hint of what was to come when she said: 'I would hate to see you dropped from the team.'

At the time, I laughed it off, saying that if I ever felt I was being kept in on sympathy, I would retire. But that last comment kept coming back to me on the train journey home. Just what, I asked myself, is happening?

During the next few days, I phoned a few close friends within the game to ask their advice. They were as puzzled and perplexed as I was – but I wanted to find out if I really was imagining that I still had plenty to offer England.

Somehow, my concern over the situation, and the fact that I had told some friends of it, got back to the officers, and a couple of weeks later I received a letter from Mollie Buckland, complaining that I had made the events of an officers' meeting common knowledge and, furthermore, that I had misinformed people. 'Thankfully', she wrote, 'I was able to give the true facts.'

Apart from stating the obvious, that I had *not* misinformed anyone, I must say that it had never occurred to me that our 'chat' in London even purported to be an 'officers' meeting'.

The letter went on: 'I am sorry that you chose to disregard the goodwill behind that meeting. We were under no obligation to travel to London at our own expense' – remember, *they* had called the meeting – 'and I shall personally think twice before suggesting such a thing again.'

So it appears that it could have been Mollie's idea to bring me to London, although her claim that there was any goodwill behind it all was, as events have proved, puzzling.

She concluded: 'While being an officer, I have made sure that your views have had a fair hearing. It is now obvious that I have not had the same treatment from you. With regrets, Mollie.'

It came through to me as a letter with a guilty conscience hung out to dry. I replied swiftly to make my position plain, and received another letter back, in which Mollie voiced her opinion that 'there is a feeling that there should be a change of captain'. Her cards, at least, were now on the table. Her letter continued:

The sole purpose of that fateful meeting was to say how we honestly thought the future of the WCA should proceed. Don't think I found it easy to suggest to you that we should have a new start with a new captain. No one appreciates more than I what you and the older! ! players have done in the past ten years. The meeting was timed to come before we had any selectors. Now they have been appointed they will have the final say in how the England squad will be trained and selected.

I could see you were hurt at the suggestion that we made, but I personally felt it was worth the risk put against the possibility of you realising what could happen and not being given the chance to step down if you wished in your own way.

When the whole story broke after the final trial match in

Halifax, I was able to look back and realise that it would not have made the slightest difference if I had scored a century every time I'd gone to the crease during 1977. The die was cast.

In fact, it was not a wildly successful summer for any of our players, myself included, although I did top-score in two trial events. And the signs that something strange was happening grew with each passing week.

A trial match was held at Dulwich during June, and I arrived a day late, still recovering from an attack of tonsilitis. I watched the second day's play, then, to prove my form and fitness, batted on the third day and scored 88, the highest score of the weekend. The teams for the next trial at Cambridge were named at the end of that day, and I was intrigued – to say the least – that I was neither captain nor vice-captain in either side. Doubly surprised, for after thirteen years representative captaincy no one had been courteous enough to say why!

The same thing happened when the teams for Halifax, the final trial, were announced after the Cambridge matches, and still there was no explanation forthcoming from the selectors – just icy looks or averted glances.

I decided I couldn't let the matter slip any further, so I went to Audrey Disbury, one of the selectors, and said, 'Can you tell me what is going on?' I explained that the attitudes of the selectors were not only upsetting me, but disturbing the atmosphere and concentration of the players taking part in the trial games. At about the same time, a deputation of England players went to see Audrey Winterbottom with a similar question, claiming that the form of many players had not been helped by this massive intrigue.

The deputation and I received the same answer: 'We are keeping our options open.' When I got home from the Cambridge match, I was visibly worried, and Derrick advised me to clarify my position with someone in control. So I phoned Rosemary Goodchild and received the assurance: 'As far as I am concerned, you are still England captain.' I accepted her at face value, but with hindsight I believe she was aware all along that I was about to be overthrown.

One would never have thought so, though, from the pleading phone call I received from Miss Goodchild during that mad mid-summer. The WCA had been let down over the sponsorship of a women v. men match to be staged at The Oval in aid of the Queen's Silver Jubilee appeal. 'Can you work a miracle for us, and get a men's team together?' she asked me – the match had to go ahead for it had been billed and the ground booked. I agreed; spent hours on the phone and collected not only a formidable team that included Australians Ian Chappell, Geoff Dymock and Mick Malone, Tony Lewis as captain and a number of Welsh rugby stars, but also a £600 sponsorship from the *Sunday Telegraph*. The match was ultimately rained off, but all the stars did turn up at The Oval, and I was ashamed that WCA made hardly any effort to provide adequate food, drinks and hospitality. I almost wished I hadn't gone to such efforts for them. Later, that wish was to become fervent.

The greatest mistake the WCA made was in selecting a successor who was not only older than me, but patently lacking in the right sort of experience. For that, they were castigated in the press. But it was not the only mistake they made.

They destroyed what little credibility they had left by refusing to comment on the news. Maybe they assumed that a 'no comment' from them would kill the story for the papers. If so, they were being very naïve. All it did was create an even greater swing of press and public sympathy my way. Eleven years in charge of a successful team cannot be ended with a 'no comment'.

More and more of the press reports suggested that my sacking was born of jealousy by the WCA officials. But the greatest irony is that if it was true, and the WCA were trying to take me out of the public eye, they had colossally misjudged the reaction. Through the sacking I gained more publicity than I had ever dreamed of – or wanted.

In the week which followed the decision, I often had to take the phone off the hook in order to sit down and have a meal. The news was local, national and international on radio, television and in newspapers. For the first time ever I featured in all the national TV news, something I had craved for – for our sport, not for myself personally.

The *Daily Express* interviewed Rosemary Goodchild, who was generally non-committal apart from one telling remark. 'I would never decry the wonderful work that Rachael has done for the Association. But she is not *the* Association.' John Morgan, the *Express* reporter, commented: 'That is the rub. Rachael did so much for women's cricket that she became women's cricket, and I suspect the ladies who are supposed to administer the game became a little bit jealous.'

On the day that the story broke, I escaped from the phone to travel to London, where I was due to take part in 'Games People Play', the BBC Radio 2 quiz programme with Peter West. It was all one tremendous rush, and I just had time to drive to the station, buy a paper and jump into the restaurant car before the train began to move. Flopping into my seat, I opened the local *Express and Star* and found myself staring at a one-inch-deep front-page headline, screaming 'TEST QUEEN RACHAEL IS SACKED'. It is the first time I've made the front page (and probably the last), and it took me completely by surprise.

That night, I was driven from the BBC Lower Regent Street recording studios to ITN, where I was interviewed live on 'News at Ten'. I'd missed the last train, but ITN chauffered me home at the end of one of the most hectic yet depressing days of my life.

Follow-ups continued throughout the next few days, and a hint of the upheavals still to come could be seen in some of the headlines. 'Storm of protest at Rachael sacking' was one; 'Now players back sacked Rachael' was another.

From two England players came particular support. Jill Cruwys was quoted as saying: 'To axe Rachael as they have done is unbelievable. She has done everything for women's cricket. Without her at the top, the sport will go down and down.' Heather Dewdney wrote to the WCA, expressing concern over the coming tour and saying of my sacking: 'It is a move which does not have the support of the majority of players available for selection.'

Perhaps the *Birmingham Evening Mail* got nearest to the point with their 19 July editorial:

With no word of explanation, not even a thank you for past services, the tight-lipped ladies of the English Women's Cricket Association sacked Rachael Heyhoe Flint as cricket captain for the winter's tour of India. Shades of 'off with her head'. So with 11 years of captaincy behind her, success in several series and a run average the envy of Geoff Boycott, the 38-year-old Wolverhampton sportswoman is dumped. The brutal dismissal of men's Test captain Brian Close a few years ago was good-natured by comparison. Mrs Flint still does not know the reason for the decision of the selectors, made after she had scored well in the trials at Halifax.

Chairman of that almost anonymous body of selectors Audrey Winterbottom will not say why: 'It was a committee decision,' she states, quietly sheathing the bloody axe. Not one member of this jolly little committee has put forward an explanation – neither has the association chairman, Rosemary Goodchild.

But there is a conclusion to be reached. Mrs Flint was far too successful for the tweed-skirt brigade, who would prefer to hide their game away, keeping it under the rigid control of so-called ladies brought up in a different fashion from the extrovert West Midlander.

Mrs Flint has made women's cricket into a sport to be taken seriously. She had done so with good humour and a flair for publicity, almost single-handed.

That is what offends the women's association. That is why they have picked a 38-year-old nobody to be the next captain. They should now do the honourable thing and speak out – or collectively resign.

On the other hand you have Tony Greig. He speaks out almost as often as Muhammad Ali, and he is in danger of being taken just about as seriously.

As it happened Greig made a fool of himself with his comments on the state of the pitch before the Old Trafford match. As a Test captain and player he has not yet acquired the judgement and dominance of someone of the quality of, yes, Rachael Heyhoe Flint.

2 Dropped

In more normal times, a match between West Midlands and Thames Valley would have been of minimal interest to anyone outside the two teams and immediate relatives. But when they met in late July 1977, dozens of spectators turned up and the match became a cold war of nerves.

The reason was very simple. This was the first match I had played since my sacking – just a week later, in fact – and one of the Thames Valley opening bowlers just happened to be the WCA chairman, Rosemary Goodchild. Naturally, the press gleefully described this as a 'High Noon' confrontation, and a bigger crowd turned up than I had ever seen at such a domestic match.

Although the chairman and I were the individuals involved, my colleagues in the West Midlands team had taken the situation to heart, and I don't think I've ever seen them more anxious to do well. Unfortunately, the game was a disater for us from start to finish. We lost chiefly through trying too hard, if that is possible, and my innings didn't get off the ground. It could have been worse, however.

I went out in my normal position at number three, and, as if we were acting an MGM film script, my first ball was bowled by Rosemary Goodchild. I played it for a single and felt gratified to hear the cheers of the crowd.

The bowler at the other end was more erratic, and the first two deliveries were 'wides'. Because of the tension I was finding it incredibly hard to concentrate. Late in the over, I groped for a ball that I should really have left alone, heard the sickening sound of an edge and turned to see the ball looping towards Rosemary Goodchild at first slip.

I don't think I could ever have lived down being caught by

her that day, and I shall always be grateful to Pauline Gibbon, the Thames Valley wicketkeeper and current England hockey goalkeeper. Taking off from her crouch position, she brilliantly dived in front of first slip and poached the catch. Although I was upset and annoyed with myself, I had been spared the complete indignity of being caught out by the chairman – again!

I have since discovered why Rosemary Goodchild bowled with such fire on that day. As the West Midlands umpire at her bowling end took the chairman's sweater as she prepared to begin, she made the following comment: 'If you want my opinion – and you're going to get it whether you want it or not – I think you've made a complete cobblers of the England captaincy!' Makes a change for an umpire to harangue a bowler: it's usually the other way round.

Not a word was spoken between Rosemary and myself throughout the afternoon and evening, and I don't think I've ever been so glad to get home from a game of cricket.

First post on Monday brought a new shock, a new insult and a new instance of the cowardice which had punctuated the WCA's treatment of this whole, sorry affair. It was a scrawled, handwritten letter from Miss Goodchild, telling me that I was not included in the England party to tour India. The letter had been posted on the Friday, but she had not had the courage or the respect to inform me of the decision verbally, despite spending the whole of Saturday afternoon in my company at the Thames Valley v. West Midlands game. I found this back-door approach unforgiveable and despicable, and the handwritten note an affront.

Despite this final insult, I laughed out loud at the text of the letter. 'The selection of a balanced team with youth in mind for the future has been of major consideration,' it stated pompously. I had a quick count and found that their youthful squad included seven girls of over thirty and very, very few in their early twenties.

So the second week of the saga began just as the first had,

with the telephone ringing non-stop as reporters sought to confirm this new twist in the tale – and I kept thinking, 'As one door closes another slams in your face!'.

The WCA made a statement through the Press Association, but it was hardly a shattering end to their official silence: 'Mary Pilling, the new captain, is a fast bowler . . . who has had experience in India.' Again, it was a laughable line, as I happened to know that Mary's 'experience' in India amounted to having passed through the country *en route* for Singapore, almost ten years earlier. I could claim to have landed at eight different Indian airports, but I don't think that would have been any more help in tackling Indian cricket than Mary's transit stop.

So in a matter of eight days I had plummetted from England captain to a club cricketer; sacked as captain, now dropped from the national squad. I was still in a daze about it all, as letters began pouring in from home and abroad. In all, I received more than two hundred, including at least one from every country in the world which plays women's cricket and two from Conservative MPs – one of which read simply: 'Ridiculous'!

Every letter I received expressed sympathy for me and anger against the decisions – except one. This little gem was from Sylvia Swinburne, the previous chairman of the WCA. She accused me of acting like a spoiled child, telling me that I should have accepted the association's decisions with good grace – and that Mary Pilling's experience in such an insanitary country would prove invaluable!

I was very grateful at this time for the chance to escape the cauldron of intrigue, and pressure, even if just for a short while. My five-day visit to Gibraltar with the BBC Radio Quiz team for 'Forces Chance', with live wires around me like Ted Moult, Neil Durden-Smith, Desmond Lyneham and producer Pat Ewing, certainly helped to heal the hurt I was feeling.

Try as I did, though, I could find no reason for accepting the WCA's unexplained decision. But, as the storm temporarily died away, I found time to reflect on the events of the previous eighteen months, and I managed to recall a number of episodes that may not exactly have endeared me to the radical and straight-laced establishment of women's cricket.

The occasion when I jokingly threatened to take the MCC to the Equal Opportunities Commission unless we could play at Lord's (explained in the next chapter), is a classic example of my doing things in just the way that the WCA detests. There were several others during 1976.

At the beginning of the cricket season, I wrote a letter to the *Daily Telegraph*, which they published, criticising Minister of Sport Dennis Howell for imposing a ban on the Ridgebacks, a Rhodesian cricket team who had hoped to tour England. It was a personal letter, stating my individual views, but the WCA insisted on reprimanding me for it.

The Australian tour of 1976 badly needed major sponsorship, and this I obtained from the food company St Ivel, thanks to a journalist contact of mine who set the wheels in motion with an advertising agency that he knew. When everything was signed and delivered, the agency asked for their normal commission. The WCA initially refused to pay, and while the two bodies haggled, I got the kickback from both sides as the go-between who had arranged it all in the first place.

When the Test series finally began, all England players were told that their children would not be allowed in the pavilions or dressing-rooms; effectively, they were not wanted on the Test grounds – their presence would disturb concentration! For much of the summer, therefore, I enlisted the help of one of our Young England players, Julie Pritchard, to look after my two-year-old son Benjamin while I played. I saw little of him during the tour until he became unwell during the Edgbaston Test. The first day's play was a Saturday, and as my home was a twenty-minute drive from the hotel, I decided I would spend the night at home. I made a secret of my plans and left the hotel when all the other players had gone to bed,

B

returning before anyone was up the next morning – play did not start until the afternoon.

During the Sunday, I was batting when I noticed Derrick, my stepson Simon, my mother, Julie Pritchard and Benjamin in the stand. I was pleased to see them and got on with my innings, thinking no more about it. But as I prepared to leave the ground at the end of the day's play, vice-chairman Mollie Buckland handed me a sealed buff envelope, without a word. I presumed it was the agenda of a meeting or some similar official business, and put it away in my pocket.

I was stopped by some traffic lights on the way back and, on an impulse, I took out the envelope, slit it open and read the note inside. It was a double reprimand this time, for the twin offences of not spending the night at the hotel and having my son on the ground. My anger, which was considerable, stemmed not so much from the reprimand – for officially I was in the wrong on both counts – but the furtive, tight-lipped manner in which it had been meted out. Can't anyone, I thought, muster enough courage to say something to my face.

The final Test of the series was at The Oval, and for a long time, Australia looked likely winners. In our second innings I needed to play the best innings of my life to save it, and I did so – 179 in eight and a half hours (the world's second-highest women's Test score), finally being caught in the last over of the game when I was trying to hit a six to finish with a flourish. As I came off, mentally and physically exhausted from the strain, the relief I felt was incredible for the game was safely drawn. I dragged myself up the steps and found Derrick waiting for me at the top. I kissed him and gratefully accepted a glass of beer. It seemed the most natural thing in the world to me, but official eyes, viewing the incident, did not approve.

Taken singly, these episodes make trivial reading, whoever was in the right and wrong. But over a period of time, they built up in the minds of the hierachy and, I believe, contributed fully to my demise.

Very few people have ever heard my true feelings on it all. I've tried to laugh it off by saying that I didn't fancy curried Christmas pudding in India anyway – and, of course, there was the consolation of spending Christmas at home with the family, and playing hockey for Staffordshire. (As it happened I might have withdrawn from the tour in any case, for my mother suffered a severe stroke in the autumn and was seriously ill.)

But I'm only kidding myself when I speak lightly of my dismissal. The whole shabby action hurt me more than I can say, particularly as it was decided on and carried out by women whom I had always counted among my friends.

I shall never forget one heart-to-heart chat I had with Audrey Winterbottom, near the end of 1976. It was an enthusiastic discussion, and she seemed as keen as I was to get the game even greater projection in 1977. After listening to my ideas, she said in her broad northern accent: 'Great, luv. We'll look forward to a smashing season next year.' On the face of it, that may seem a most inconsistent comment, although I will never know for sure if Audrey was taking orders from above when she told me I was fired.

The rank-and-file support from the players which had built up behind me led eventually to a call for an Extraordinary General Meeting. Ten member clubs, as required in the constitution, called the meeting with the motion that 'This meeting should discuss and vote on the resolution that they disapprove of the manner in which the England captaincy was handled.' A trivial technicality delayed the meeting, but it was eventually fixed, fittingly enough, for Guy Fawkes Day. It was held at Maidenhead, scarcely accessible from the north of England, but more than two hundred people turned up – a far bigger attendance than for any general meeting in my memory.

I was very thrilled that the resolution was carried, by an overwhelming 107–46, but the clear vote of 'no confidence' was totally ignored by the selectors. Only two of them were present, neither spoke, and no one had the spirit to resign.

The press and BBC Television News were there in force, and afterwards I spoke to them before rushing back to Wolverhampton to take part in a local 'Superstars' contest – just the sort of thing, as one journalist pointed out, that the WCA were not happy about.

Bitterness for my lot or immodesty do not come into it when I say that the WCA have surely done their cause harm by their ham-handed tactics. There can be no clearer proof of that than the fact that Jack Hayward resigned his patronage of the WCA in January 1978 on the grounds that they had sabotaged all the work that he and I had put into the game over the past four years. Before the sacking, Jack had offered to pay the costs of the England squad to India. When he heard the story, he withdrew his support. How many Jack Haywards are there in the world that the WCA can afford to alienate them by unexplained actions?

As for me, the urge to seek reinstatement is past, but the wound is still painful. Forgetting that it is I who is personally involved, it is still disturbing that a player has been dropped who yet commands a place on merit in an England side. My sacking as captain may have been a matter of unanimous opinion among the selectors; my axing from the side is something else, and records prove that my form in the most recent Test series was better than in any other and also better than that of any other England player.

I hate carping; I hate sounding bitter; and, who knows, perhaps I could make a late comeback in my forties to the England team in the style of Cyril Washbrook, Denis Compton and Brian Close. But whatever the establishment of the WCA may have achieved, they can never take away from me the love I have for the game of cricket; they can never take away the friends I have made throughout the world in sport, the media and show business; they can never take away my MBE, awarded for services to women's cricket; and they can never take away the host of happy memories I have to look back on.

3 Lord's

Early in 1976, I made a semi-serious remark to a national newspaper journalist and unwittingly flung myself into an episode that was to deepen dramatically my conflict with the Women's Cricket Association. My jocular quote grew out of a chat I was having with *Daily Mirror* sports writer Frank Taylor on the continuing rebuffs in our attempts to persuade Lord's to stage a women's match.

The subject, at that time, was very dear to my heart because I had been appointed eighteen months earlier as the WCA's promotional go-between in advance of the 1976 Australian visit that was to mark the Association's fiftieth anniversary. A match at Lord's would be our greatest selling-point to the media and sponsors, as I was acutely aware, and I had aimed most of my efforts to that end – going so far as to make an unscheduled and completely irregular visit to the MCC offices at Lord's to confront secretary Jack Bailey towards the end of 1975.

I am sure Mr Bailey is not the sort of person who welcomes people 'popping in' unannounced on business, and when I saw him he was polite but firmly non-committal in answer to my harassment. No, he said, he could not promise anything. Apart from the various committees (here we go again!) that would have to approve the game, it had to be remembered that the Lord's square was being re-laid and they were looking to reduce rather than increase the volume of fixtures. He followed up with a letter saying basically the same thing, and as no further progress seemed to have been made, I was understandably beginning to despair by the time 1975 was coming to an end. It was in December of that year, five months before our Jubilee Cricket Tour, that I attended a Sports Council reception and began chatting to Frank Taylor.

Frank asked if there were any new developments in our Lord's ambitions and I gave him a moody negative. Then, though why it should suddenly have occurred to me I can't imagine, I half-jokingly added: 'There are a lot of sex discrimination cases in the news these days – I think I'll take Lord's to the Equal Opportunities Commission!'

It was the sort of line that no journalist worth his salt would have ignored. To be honest, I don't think I even wanted it ignored at the time, and sure enough, Frank phoned me at home the following day to check that it was all right for him to make a story out of it.

I agreed, although deep down, I knew that I never had the slightest intention of carrying out the threat, or indeed the capability. The cost of such an action would have stretched my finances far more than even Lord's, although, in retrospect, they may now think it a cheap option after the quarter of a million pounds that Kerry Packer's action cost them!

To be fair to our cause, I hoped that Frank's story did not appear as a completely outrageous take-over bid on our part. I pointed out that we did not necessarily want a Test match at Lord's. A one-day international was the limit of our demands and we were willing to reorganise our entire season around it – even if Lord's offered us a date in February or November!

The story appeared the next morning, bigger than I had envisaged it. The reaction was bigger still. The phone got me out of bed and scarcely stopped all day. Radio news programmes, chat shows, every national paper and agency in England seemed eager to follow up the tale of this one-woman stand against the 'chauvinist bounders' of the St John's Wood headquarters of cricket. It quickly became obvious to me that the whole thing had got out of hand. I had never wanted it to grow into that kind of national issue, but when it did, I was in an impossible position. If I went on, I realised it could upset and even alienate the sensitive men of Lord's. If I said I had never really meant it and it was all a crazy joke I would have wasted the intention behind my tongue-in-cheek threat. I decided that the merry-go-round was travelling too fast, but I couldn't get off.

The following day's newspaper coverage was even more striking. Lord's had been approached for their reaction, as had the WCA. And it was at this stage in the chapter that the size of my clanger came home to me.

Completely unknown to me, the WCA had been negotiating with Lord's, in a quiet and correct manner, for some time. My actions had certainly not helped the cause, might indeed have sabotaged it. The WCA were livid – and quite understandably so. Yet I was at a total loss to understand why they had kept these discussions a complete secret from the very person whom they had put in charge of WCA promotions for the summer; had I known I would never have floated my threats to the press. I never received a satisfactory answer to that question, only the obvious impression that they had, for reasons of their own, not wanted me to be involved.

Illogically, the situation simply got worse when I discovered that all was not lost and that we had, indeed, been granted a day at Lord's for the final one-day international of the summer. Again, I must stress that I was in the dark. I didn't have a clue that a decision on the match had been made until another pre-breakfast phone call, from the Press Association, one morning in May informed me that the date had been confirmed. They wanted my reaction, naturally enough, and they weren't the only ones. It was that January morning all over again, with the radio stations phoning for a live quote about pouring champagne on the cornflakes and all the papers coming on for some ecstatic comment.

My delight, my triumphant smile and my happy quotes dominated the newspaper stories. I hadn't designed it that way. I hadn't asked all the papers to phone me up and nor had I told them to ignore the part played by senior WCA officials, which, regrettably, is what happened. Most important, I had *not* leaked the story to the papers, because, I repeat, I had not known anything to leak. Sadly, certain members of the WCA hierachy just did not believe me. I think they saw it as a deliberate attempt on my part to harvest all the praise that was coming.

The match was big news for about a week, and throughout that time, the then WCA chairman and number-one negotiator, Sylvia Swinburne, hardly gathered a single mention. Unfortunate, because she undoubtedly deserved it, but it's a fact of life that administrators are not necessarily newspaper's targets.

Just to stir the antagonism a little more, another controversy now arose over television rights for the Lord's game. It ended in unpleasantness, and, almost inevitably it seems, I was again involved. This one dated back almost two years, to October of 1974. Having been given promotional responsibilities for the 1976 season, I went to see my old friends John Bromley and Stuart McConachie, the powers-that-be behind ITV's 'World of Sport'. I gauged their interest in covering a match at Lord's in 1976, which at that time was nothing more than hypothetical – a dream.

After consulting their schedules, John and Stuart wrote to me confirming their interest and advising that a date in August, well clear of other summer sport highspots, would be preferable for the final match, whether the game was at the original venue of Sunbury CC; Lord's or Timbuktoo!

By February of 1976, when I next met them, I was despairing of winning the fight with Lord's. But, over a claret-filled lunch at the London Weekend TV headquarters, I managed to get 'World of Sport' to agree to cover the final match of the tour, wherever it was staged. At that point, the final game was scheduled for Sunbury, and I felt fairly pleased with myself as I reported to Sylvia Swinburne about my little coup by phone and letter. She accepted the news gratefully.

The next part of the story is necessarily hazy as I cannot be certain of the sequence of events. All I do know is that shortly after Lord's agreed to host us for a day, the WCA spoke to the BBC and negotiated a deal with *them* for coverage of the game. I was not informed of this development until the tour was under way, in fact not until after the final day of the opening Test match against Australia in June, and at first I found it hard to believe the matter-of-fact manner in which I was told. Now, I just find it impossible to forgive. The association, through its chairman, had been kept fully in touch with my efforts and my progress in obtaining an agreement with ITV in February. It seems they chose to ignore etiquette and committed the basic business-crime of taking agreed trade to the opposition.

It goes without saying that 'World of Sport' were furious, and, fortunately, understood completely that I had played no part in any deception. They were not prepared to stand back and accept defeat with a polite bow, however, and John Bromley, chief executive of 'World of Sport', composed a stinging letter to the WCA. He also sent me a copy, which I have kept. The tone is angry, though never impolite, and the overwhelming message is that ITV will never again consider covering a women's cricket match. He wrote: 'I am most distressed that she [R.H.F.] should be placed in such an embarrassing situation by the inefficiency of certain WCA officials. I would like to make it clear that following our recent dealings with the WCA we will certainly not be in a hurry to cover or promote women's cricket in 'World of Sport' in the future.' Another battle lost.

With all this going on, it would have been easy for me to lose sight of the fact that the greatest ambition of my cricket career was about to be realised. Certainly, the widening rift caused me a lot of sadness, but I remained determined that it would not ruin the thrill of actually playing at Lord's – the holy of holies.

My problems were not over, however. We reported to Lord's on the eve of the match for a practice session in the Nursery End nets. As usual, I was wearing my Adidas training shoes with three green stripes running down them, and I was both amused and startled when our association's vice-chairman fussed up to me in the early minutes of our practice, whipped a tube of shoe whitening furtively out of her handbag, and immediately stooped to erase my stripes. It was a rule of Lord's and the Test and County Cricket Board that cricketers should not wear advertising material on clothing, and I was in the wrong. But the furtive, panicking manner in which I was put to rights was laughable.

It was also symptomatic of the attitude which persisted among our officials in the days and hours leading up to the match. Despite the fact that we were all adult and experienced cricketers, and most of us had conducted ourselves admirably on several full-length overseas tours, we were followed around as if they all believed we were at least planning to blow up the Old Father Time on his pavilion perch!

Another thing that annoyed me was the starchy official attitude to two pictures which appeared in two different national papers, for which I was blamed. One was used on the morning of the match, showing me with baby Benjamin. Throughout the practice session, Benjamin plus babysitter Julie had stayed behind the ropes surrounding the nets. I didn't even know they were there until the end of our stint, when I naturally went over to them. One of the photographers present asked if he could take a picture of mother and baby. I saw nothing against it and agreed. When it appeared, I was accused of publicising 'the wrong image'.

The other picture was in the *Daily Express*, the day after the Australians had practised at Lord's earlier in the tour. It hit the Photo News page, was spread across the full six columns and showed the Australians in various stages of undress in the make-shift changing-rooms. The Lord's authorities brought this inadvertently on themselves by making the players change in the public ladies' cloakroom. The alert *Daily Express* photographer, Hilaria McCarthy, noticed this, nipped in to spend a penny, snapped and nipped out again! And I got the blame – quite unfairly, as I had had nothing to do with it.

We stayed at the Westmoreland Hotel, on the perimeter of Lord's, for the night before the match, but despite the comfort of the place I hardly slept at all. Once again, the nerves that many refuse to believe I possess were forcing themselves forward. I was so concerned that the day to come should be the greatest possible success, for I knew that this, more than any other occasion we had ever been part of, was a searching trial of women's cricket.

I got up early for breakfast – just toast and coffee: butterflies wouldn't have let bacon and egg settle! I then looked forward to the first thrill of the day – an unhindered passage through the famous Grace Gates at Lord's. Many was the occasion that I had had to plead my way through – I reckon it's easier to get into Fort Knox than Lord's – but not this time. I drove my car up to the gates, all required passes glued to the windscreen, and as the gateman waved me on I raised my cine-camera and recorded the moment – I almost shouted out 'Hallelujah'!

Inside the pavilion, men seemed to be stationed on every corner of every stairway, just to ensure that we didn't encroach on forbidden territory. We were shown warily into our dressing-room and my first impression was how incredibly antique the room looked.

Perhaps I was looking through domesticated female eyes at

"I knew it! Letting 'em play cricket at Lord's was the thin edge of the wedge."

a male domain, but to me the cranky old wash-basins, floors of erupting linoleum, torn chairs and not-so-sweet-smelling loos merely emphasised what an age-old place Lord's is.

It wasn't until I stepped out on to the player's balcony that the aura of the ground really hit me. This was the balcony that I had viewed so many times from below, staring at idols of the male game. Now it was our place, I must say I felt extremely proud.

Our two attendants, women of course, brought in some English roses – surely an innovation for the day, I thought: Greig and Brearley don't order these, do they? Then it was time to toss up, and my first walk of the day into the centre of the arena.

I lost the toss which ironically turned out to be a stroke of good fortune for England. Australia, a match up in the one-day series, elected to bat first. They had not bargained for the early movement of the ball in the Lord's atmosphere, which was just as well, for neither had I. I would have batted first, too!

In a way, I was pleased that we were forced to field, for at least it meant that I would be the first woman ever to step on to the Lord's turf in a playing capacity. That meant more to me than I can say, even if I did do it wrong. Instead of turning left at the foot of the stairs, I opted to go straight on, out through the double doors, then along the pavilion frontage to the steps on to the grass, simply because no one had told us if we were allowed into the Long Room or not. The last thing I wanted to do at such a late stage was commit an irretrievable faux pas.

There were quite a few spectators in the ground early on, as well as plenty of cameramen. One of them asked me to raise my arm in a victory salute as I walked on. I refused, intent on doing nothing that could possibly offend the Lord's authorities who had finally shown us the green light.

My feelings as I actually walked on the pitch were of elation, pride, misgivings and extreme nervousness. I felt goosepimples appearing as we walked out to the middle and I know it sounds rather like Angela Brazil, but I could have easily cried.

I was surprised how cosy it was at Lord's compared with the wide open vastness of Old Trafford and The Oval, the concrete coolness of the Edgbaston Test Ground, and the extreme width of Trent Bridge.

I was surprised how much the field sloped from one side to the other and it took some time for us to adapt to the speed with which the ball ran down to the Tavern. Fortunately, it took the Australians longer to adjust to the complete occasion. We dismissed their most dangerous bat, Lorraine Hill (who had scored 1,000 runs, including five centuries, on the tour), inside the first over, and never really looked back.

Eventually we were left to score only 169 in our fifty overs, and were given a start which virtually guaranteed us victory in the game. It was not, however, likely to be quick enough to give us the fastest overall scoring rate in the series, which matched against Australia's win at Canterbury three days previously, would have won us the St Ivel Cream Jug. So, I was left with a decision – do we go for the win at Lord's, or risk everything – and possibly lose – by throwing the bat and try to take the series. I put it to the team, and they supported my secret personal view by opting for the win at Lord's. We did so comfortably, by eight wickets, but some officials annoyed me again by showing some resentment at the fact that we had not brought home the trophy.

When I went in to bat I scuttled nervously through the Long Room, smiling a pale thank you to the shouts of good luck. I reached the middle, took guard and surveyed the Australians field placings; I then drew breath to relax. The cloistered silence clung all around like a blanket; there was an air of expectancy. Suddenly from out of the reverent hush came Benjamin's piping tones – 'I can see you Mummy,' and I smiled, drew breath, relieved. I was relaxed and ready!

For me, the greatest part of the occasion arrived at its climax. I had been batting with Chris Watmough when she struck the winning runs, and the crowd, which had built remarkably to about 8,000 during the day, stood to a man (and woman) and roared approval as we came off.

In the pavilion, age-old members creaked to their feet, shouting 'Encore!' and 'Bravo!'. Cheers rang through the Long Room as I ran up the pavilion steps two at a time. It was the sort of moment that made me want to call for an instant 'Match of the Day' replay. Champagne flowed in our dressing-room – a gift from the *Sunday Telegraph* for my 179 at the Oval; we drank out of teacups!

Sadly, though, it was all over, and a day that had been planned for so long, and caused me so much personal aggravation, had to end with a disappointment. With thousands of happy, patriotic spectators waiting outside for the presentation, the establishment insisted that the trophy and awards should be handed over in the Long Room, where there was barely room for even the teams and officials. Lord's said bleakly that there was no precedent for making a presentation on the pitch. Had they forgotten every male cricketing cup final? Not even the players' relatives were allowed into the Long Room to share with us all the thrill of the whole occasion – they were left outside in anti-climax, waiting like the peasants outside the castle. It seemed to me very sad that Lord's should show such an unsympathetic lack of public relations, for many of our supporters had travelled hundreds of miles to be with us on Ladies' Day there.

4 Opening the Innings

My first brush with the police taught me that men have little regard for women cricketers, and my immediate instinct was to register protest. It happened early in my childhood – I think I was eight years old – while I was engaged in my customary tomboy habit of playing with my brother Nicholas and his friends.

The road where I grew up was in a quiet suburb of Wolverhampton, and as there was so little traffic, the road became our sports arena. While the girls of the neighbourhood tended their dolls and prams, I preferred to play bicycle polo – a fraught, high-speed version of the royal's game – and soccer and cricket with the lads.

On this infamous occasion when I brushed with the law, we were some way through an intense cricket match in the road, when one of the local bobbies drove up. He marched towards us as we rushed for cover: aware that our games were at least frowned upon, if not illegal, we scattered to hiding-places behind various trees and hedges. The arm of the law yanked us all out one by one, however, and then out came the black notebook and pencil. He took the names and addresses of all the boys and then went to replace his notebook in his pocket. This was too much for me. I reached up, tapped him on the shoulder and pointed out that I had been playing cricket, too. His answer was most pitying: 'Girls don't play cricket,' which was about as devastating a blow to my pride as anyone could have delivered.

Dixon of Dock Green himself could not have changed my ways, though, and our games went on as if the police had never interrupted. At that stage of my life, I was as keen on football as anything else, and took every chance available to play as well as watch the game.

When I was eleven, my school organised a weekend camp. One of the activities was a football match, and of twenty-two children on the field I was the solitary female. One of the masters was bright enough to take a photograph and it appeared in our local paper the next week. There I was, pigtails flapping, thumping over a corner, with the caption: 'So you thought football was a boy's game, did you?'

A few years before that, I had even been given a football as a Christmas present. I was about seven, and still had a halfbelief in Father Christmas sufficient to keep me awake through the night as Christmas Day arrived. Eventually, a shadowy figure crept into my bedroom and placed a large parcel at the foot of my bed. I hardly waited for 'Santa' to leave the room before leaping out of bed to make the joyful discovery that I had a real, leather football. At 3.30 that morning I pummelled my older brother Nicholas awake and dragged him out on to the lawn for a pre-dawn football match!

It would, retrospectively, have been odd if I had grown up with no enthusiasm for sport, for it was firmly in my blood. Both my parents were physical education specialists, and proficient at various sports in their own right. Geoffrey Heyhoe, my Norfolk-born father, and Roma Crocker, my mother, who was born in Bristol but lived most of her early life in Hampshire, were in fact brought together by Silkeborg PE college in Copenhagen. Father had studied there in the early 1920s, and when he returned as a lecturer two or three years later, my mother had arrived as a student. Much of my spirit of adventure must have derived from mother, who may have been considered a very unusual woman in the 1920s. The place of the woman was very definitely in the home in those days, so to snub the tradition and qualify as a PE teacher required some spirit. To do so in Denmark was even more remarkable. Both my parents had considerable skill in tennis and hockey, and Father even played soccer for a Denmark Amateur XI while in Copenhagen, so the chances of my becoming an opera singer must always have been slim.

Above: 1 A portly RHF, aged two. I guess my parents put me out in the garden to scare away the birds. *Below left:* 2 My father, Geoffrey Heyhoe. His nose had a confrontation with a hockey ball. *Below right:* 3 Sweetness and innocence as a twelve-year-old bridesmaid at my cousin's Hampshire wedding. Rumour had it that I wore hockey boots under my dress!

4 Dame Anna Neagle stars in another role at the Oval with a very experienced cast of extras, 1963. Dame Anna is an honorary member of the WCA

5 The Hon. Angus Ogilvy greets the England hockey team at Wembley in 1964. He was more nervous than the players, watched by a predominantly female audience of a mere 60,000

Above: 6 'All three fought for their country.' The late Lt.Gen. Sir Oliver Leese, president of the MCC and Warwickshire, who succeeded Lord Montgomery in North Africa, talks to Mike Smith, England and Warwickshire captain, and RHF in Edgbaston County Cricket Ground dining-room, 1964. *Below:* 7 'Things go better with Coca-Cola,' but no one is drinking it at a Coca-Cola reception in 1966. Left to right: a Coca-Cola director; Trish McKelvey, New Zealand captain; the late Sir Oliver Leese; a smoking RHF and Richie Benaud, one of Australia's great captains

8 Joyce Grenfell gives a
'stately as a galleon' interview
to one of her most ardent
admirers for the
Wolverhampton Chronicle

9 A Sober moment? RHF and
Gary Sobers watching a
cricket match in Dunedin,
New Zealand, in 1969

Both father and mother returned to England to take up teaching posts in Yorkshire, and didn't meet again until 1930 – at a reunion of the Silkeborg College, held in Leeds. Two years later, they were married.

By the time I came on the scene in 1939, my father had become an organiser of physical education in Staffordshire and my parents had moved from their first marital home, in Leicester, to my childhood town of Wolverhampton.

Woodfield Avenue School, in Penn, was the first school of my life, and it was there that I found myself showing a real interest in games for the first time. Rounders and netball introduced me to team games and I felt a real desire to be among the best and play in the school team, as well as the boys' cricket and football teams. My competitive urges are perhaps best illustrated by my reaction when losing the obstacle race on school sports day. As captain of the 'Reds', I was in a clear lead, cheered on by parents and pupils, until I reached the stage where we had to walk along an upturned form. I fell off, the race was lost and I spent the rest of that evening in floods of tears.

Although I devoted little time to academic matters, I managed to pass the eleven-plus exam and graduate to Wolverhampton Girls' High School, a twist of good fortune as it was a school with a long and strong sporting tradition. I spent most school days, however, eagerly looking forward to the evenings and weekends, which were for me dominated by sport. At first, it would simply be playing mock-up games with my brother and his friends, but as I grew older I began to enjoy watching my father play. In the winter, he was a cunning, skilful player with Wolverhampton Hockey Club and I would go around with him to all the grounds, invariably insisting that he and his team-mates indulge in a match with me, both at half-time and when the game was over. Summer meant cricket, and I have fond memories of packing up a picnic lunch or tea and setting off with Father in the car. From a very early age I took along my own scorebook and pencil, and it was rumoured that I could score a cricket match competently before I could even string a sentence together in a school book.

I was only eleven when I went along to watch father playing cricket for the Technical College on a day when they were one man short. Amazingly, I soon found myself marked down to bat at number eleven for the college and had to go out to the crease to stave off defeat. The pads reached my waist and the bat felt like a tree trunk, but the men were kind enough to bowl me a few slowish half-volleys, and to everyone's surprise I managed to score two or three undefeated runs and save the game.

Back at school, I was chiefly restricted to the orthodox girls' games – hockey and netball in the winter, tennis and rounders in the summer. But things began to change when Lancashire-born Mary Greenhalgh, a representative cricket and hockey player, arrived to take charge of our PE department. In the summer of 1954, she took a somewhat rebellious school party to the Edgbaston Test ground to watch the Midland women's team play the touring New Zealanders. This was euphoria for me. Not only were we missing school lessons to watch cricket, but it was women's cricket, played at a very high standard.

As I studied the game that day at Edgbaston, I made up my mind that this was the life for me. Afterwards, we were allowed to go and meet the New Zealanders, and the autographs I avidly collected are still in my possession today. But I came away with more than signatures. I came away with an image of an exciting, challenging life, travelling the world playing cricket, meeting people. It seemed everything I wanted out of life, and I think it was there and then that I determined I must play cricket for England women – though, if the truth were known, I wasn't even sure whether England had a women's cricket team!

Looking back now at the team photograph of the 1954 Wolverhampton Girl's School cricket XI, it is interesting to find that I am one of three girls who in fact went on to play for England – an extraordinary achievement for a single school. The other two were Jackie Elledge and Ann Jago (known to us all as Sago), great friends of mine long after we had all left schooldays behind.

If this was in fact the time when I decided my future, I certainly lacked nothing in the way of support and encouragement. My parents were, I believe, genuinely pleased at the sporting direction I had chosen, and my father would often spend hours bowling at me in the garden.

Our house seemed to be adopted as the sporting Mecca by the entire adolescent population of the road, but even when alone, I was never lost for something to do. I devised my own method of solitary practice, suspending a cricket ball on string from an overhanging plank attached to a low gutter, and patiently drove the ball backwards and forwards until my arms ached and the gutter nearly fell off.

Brother Nicholas and his friends at first tried to exclude me from their back-lawn cricket matches. For some time, I was delegated as preserver of the flower beds. In other words, they deigned to let me field, but refused me the chance to either bat or bowl.

After serving my apprenticeship in the covers, however, they relented and allowed me an innings, presumably with the conviction that it wouldn't last long anyway. I shocked them all by batting undefeated for three days and accumulating a score of about 380 not out. By the end of it, they were so frustrated – I think pride came into it, too – that they declared the opening of the football season and switched games, despite the fact that it was only mid-June.

Being four years older, Nicholas was able to bully little sister quite successfully. But he did, at least, teach me a great deal about courage.

I had to put up with such harrowing indignities as having the vacuum cleaner held over my head so that my plaits were sucked up to the machine. I had to join in crazy 'dares', which included jumping off a twelve-foot-high balcony on to a mattress on our lawn – only when our parents were out, of course.

Nicholas also involved me in his cycle speedway team, which he called the Penn Rockets, and he taught me how to ride a motor-bike. At least, he showed me how to operate clutch, gears and throttle and launched me off over the fields near our home. What he had omitted to explain was how to work the brakes!

Eventually, I became accepted by his mates, almost as one of the gang, although they insisted on nicknaming me Lizzie after that obnoxious Violet Elizabeth Bott in the 'Just William' books who was always threatening to 'scweam and scweam until I'm sick'. To them, I had several uses, not the least important of which involved being sent round to neighbours' houses to retrieve lost cricket balls and footballs, exerting all my feminine charm!

The family on one side of us grew tired of our games and would often refuse to return the ball. But that was almost a relief compared with the house on the other side, where the people were friendly enough but their fearsome vicious bulldog would threaten permanent damage to anyone who set foot on his territory. Duelling with that dog certainly sharpened up my reflexes – as it would have done for anyone whose job it was to bend down and find cricket balls under the rhododendrons with a snarling, snapping creature bearing down on one's seat at a rate of knots.

The garden games involved a simple system of scoring runs, including six if you cleared a fence or hit the house wall on the full or twelve if you cleared the roof. If you broke a window, however, you were out! Not only that, but you also abandoned your part in the game to race into town by bicycle and collect the necessary replacement pane of glass before my parents could discover any damage. I think our local glazier must have been familiar with every window pane in our house, and several surrounding houses, by the time we had grown up.

When in the sixth form at school I scored the first century

of my career. It was against Bilston High School, and I still have the press-cutting to remind me that at one point I struck three sixes and a four in a single over, though admittedly the boundaries were very short. The cutting also reports that it was the first century recorded by a pupil of my school and that I followed it up by taking six wickets for seven runs in the same match. All good, ego-building stuff to reflect on.

Despite my reasonably rapid progress at the game, I retained a very schoolgirlish attitude. In 1955, at sixteen years old, I played my first senior county match for Staffordshire, against Warwickshire. I took six wickets but got myself run out for only seven runs. The most eye-catching feature I found when consulting the match scorecard, however, was the note I had penned in at the top. It reads: 'LUNCH – salad, cheese and biscuits, squash (iced). TEA – sandwiches, lemonade, cream cakes (four).' Pig!

Saturdays were now a crazy rush throughout the year, with a school match in the morning followed by a club fixture in the afternoon, either for Wolverhampton Women's Cricket Club in the summer or Tettenhall Ladies' Hockey Club in the winter. I couldn't have managed the schedule but for the selfless aid of my parents, who always collected me from my morning game, rushed me home for a hurried bite of lunch and ferried me off again to the club match. It makes me tired now just to think of playing all that sport in a single day, but with youth on my side it seemed nothing at all.

I had started out in hockey as a speedy right-winger, but one day at school, I volunteered to play in goal, perhaps because I idolised the Wolves goalkeeper Bert Williams. My instinct for the position was no doubt assisted by the kicking ability I had developed through countless fiery football matches with my brother, and since that day I have never considered another switch. At the time of writing, I am into my twenty-third season as Staffordshire's goalkeeper.

The school encouraged us to watch as much top-class sport as possible, and Mary Greenhalgh, the sports mistress I admired so much, decided that we should go down to Wembley Stadium for the annual women's hockey international.

I remember going to four internationals, all convincingly won by England, but the first trip was easily the most memorable. It was St Trinian's outing at its best and it makes me shudder now just to recall some of the things we got up to.

My mother packed me a huge picnic for the train journey to Wembley, but I'd eaten the lot by the time we reached Birmingham, thirty minutes from Wolverhampton! On the way down to London, we picked up various other school parties from different towns, and the noise was quite unbelievable.

One of the more foolish games we played on the train could easily have been disastrous. Our party occupied the end carriage, and it seemed a fun idea for two of us to lean out of opposite windows at the back and stretch round to wave to each other behind the train. What would have happened if a train had passed travelling in the opposite direction just doesn't bear thinking about.

We all thought ourselves very bold and grand, drinking from lemonade bottles on the train, but a story relayed to me by a BBC reporter shows how times can change in the space of twenty years. In 1975, the BBC apparently sent a camera crew from Manchester to London to film a school party bound for the hockey international. Instead of lemonade, these teenage schoolgirls were heavily armed with vodka. But at the end of the trip, far from showing signs of being inebriated, they were seen carrying off their PE master – drunk and horizontal!

At seventeen, I made my second trip to Ramsgate with the Staffordshire side for the Midland Inter-counties New Year hockey festival, and at the end of it, I was astonished to find myself named in the Midlands reserve team.

That was clearly the most significant step I had yet made towards international status, and coupled with my development within cricket, I suppose it represented a good reason for my sports-minded parents to feel proud. They did retain a strong interest and identity with my progress, but thankfully they refused to become the doting, blinkered types who can see nobody but their own child and end up doing him or her far more harm than good.

On one occasion during my early days in the county cricket team, however, I must have had every chance of benefiting by their presence for in that match my father was umpiring and my mother was scoring!

It was important that I did not become monopolised by sport, although I may not have thought so at the time, and I am now appreciative of the practical knowledge I derived from joining the Girl Guides. My enjoyment of the activities of this organisation was further proof that I was more practical than academic, and my guiding career reached a happy climax when I became a Queen's Guide at sixteen.

I suppose much of my social life revolved around school and sports clubs but I didn't want it any other way. There had always been boys in my life from the early days of joining in games with my brother's friends, but I was never the dizzy teenage girl for whom the only important thing in life was to find a boyfriend and cling on to him. If I had reached sixteen without a boyfriend I would certainly not have gone into fits of depression and considered myself to be 'on the shelf', which seems to be an increasing trend these days.

Other than sport, my interests at school tended towards music and drama. I was given crazy character parts in school plays (The Mock Turtle in *Alice in Wonderland*, for example; the Jackdaw in *The Jackdaw of Rheims*), and I sang in the concerts. But I was so badly affected by stage nerves that during one Christmas concert I accidentally destroyed a rendition of 'We three Kings of Orient are'. I was down to sing the part of the second king but in a moment of pure panic, I simply repeated the verse that the first king had just sung, much to the cringing embarrassment of my parents in their front-row seats.

I also played the part of the wicked sorceress when we gave a public performance of the opera *Dido and Aeneas,* and had to sing seventy-two bars, solo! The thing was doomed to failure, though, from the time our orchestra's lead violinist returned from the first interval, sat down too heavily on her chair and disconnected the light over her sheet music. The middle act was consequently something of a farce with a scratchy and discordant noise coming from the violin area as the poor girl tried vainly to read her music.

I still retain a great love for music, and I have a secret desire to sing 'Rule Britannia' with a full orchestra in the Royal Albert Hall on the last night of the Proms. I gather that I can sing fairly melodically, so perhaps I might be able to burst forth on the wings of song one fine day – stand by for blasting!

Another great passion in my life is Wolverhampton Wanderers Football Club, and I shall never forget the May day in 1949 when they won the FA Cup. We had no tickets and there was no television, but the entire family crowded around the wireless at home and listened intently to every minute of the Cup Final commentary, finally breaking into whoops of delight at Wolves' 3–1 win over Leicester City.

That evening, I ran round to our local newsagents to be among the first to buy a copy of the commemorative *Express and Star,* printed on gold paper to honour the Wolves' colours. I've still got it today – the front page carrying a five-inch-deep headline which simply announces 'IT'S OURS'.

I went to Wolves' home matches at Molineux whenever I could, sometimes with my parents and often just with my brother. I was present in their great days, when floodlights were introduced and they celebrated with memorable matches against legendary continental sides such as Honved, Spartak and Moscow Dynamo.

Billy Wright, the marvellous, blond centre-half, was everybody's hero, but in addition to him my own special idol was 'The Cat', goalkeeper Bert Williams. When Bert retired, he opened a sports shop in Wolverhampton, and I got to know him well enough to take a holiday job as an assistant, serving customers, repairing hockey sticks and cricket bats, blowing up footballs, etc. I loved the work, of course, and it had its outside benefits as Bert supplied me with all the hockey and cricket kit I needed.

The Wolves match I shall never forget was when they played Blackpool at the peak of Stanley Matthews' era of mastery. Such was the lure of this magical footballer that Nicholas, my father and I queued outside for hours before the gates opened, and I was almost crushed in the huge crowd. We eventually got in, Nicholas carrying a building brick for me to stand on as I was so small – imagine his being allowed to carry such a potentially offensive projectile into a football ground nowadays, and the reaction from the law if he said the brick was for his sister to stand on! I remember nothing about the result, but I have a clear recollection of seeing Matthews play, and of staring at a completely drunken fan who seemed to be cheering for both sides but identified himself as a Blackpool supporter by the piece of tangerine peel in his buttonhole.

Back home, I became familiar with another pastime unusual among females by the presence of a snooker table in our family house. I found both billiards and snooker enjoyable, which was more than our dining-room wall did. It was so close to the table on one side that anyone drawing back the cue at all swiftly was bound to plant another dent in the plaster.

Coincidentally, there is also a billiards room in my married home, and I often take on husband Derrick at snooker. Even here, however, my competitive nature gets the better of me and I will never close an evening's snooker until I have won a game. I often think that Derrick lets me win so he can get some sleep.

As the end of my school life drew closer, however, the need to study for exams increased daily. I found it all a bit of a bind, particularly as these important exams always clashed with both the Test matches and Wimbledon. In the upper sixth, when the exams were over, I even played truant for a day to watch the Edgbaston Test against the 1957 West Indies, and was rewarded for my crime by seeing Peter May and Colin Cowdrey complete their record-breaking fourth-wicket stand of 411 against the genius of Ramadhin and Valentine.

Somehow, I gathered together seven O-level passes and an English A-level, but, as is the case with so many other people, I often now regret that I didn't devote more time and attention to academic matters. The only career I ever had in mind was teaching PE, partly through the influence of my parents and partly through my admiration for Mary Greenhalgh at my own school.

I applied to Dartford College of Physical Education and was summoned to be interviewed by the principal, Edith Alexander. I don't think she would have minded me calling her slightly eccentric – she certainly gave every indication of being so during the interview. After the expected questions on sporting background and achievement, she mentioned that she had noticed from my application that I was interested in music. What standard did I reach in piano playing, she asked? And what was my main piece? When I told her that it was Handel's Largo (Grade 2, failed version!), she asked me to sing it to her, and the cacophany that followed makes it even more of a miracle that I was accepted.

Accepted I was, though, and with thoughts of the career at Dartford looming, the final school weeks lost significance. The headmistress made me a prefect for the closing six weeks of term, pointedly announcing that it was in recognition of my services to school sport rather than for any other qualities – and I have to confess the privilege failed to check my extrovert ways.

I finished school life in a grand manner. My boyfriend of the time was studying in Bristol and had loaned me his motorscooter between weekends. I felt very smug about riding into school every day, but on my final day I took it a step further and rode the Lambretta, albeit gingerly, along the school's corridors – the secret is out at last!

Sometimes, when I look back, I think that most people at Wolverhampton Girls' High must have been quietly relieved to see the back of me.

5 Touring

Never the model student, I continued to be Rachael the
Rebel during my three-year course at Dartford. Many was
the time I could be found shuffling uncomfortably on the
principal's carpet while she reprimanded me stiffly for one
misdemeanour or another.

Perhaps the most crazy offence I committed was on the
afternoon when I decided to test the fire escape in my room. I
lived on the top floor of a tower block in the college, and the
belt and sling appliance provided looked pretty inadequate.
So, as it was a sunny Sunday and there was little else to do, I
took a few of my friends into the room to conduct an ex-
periment. A girl named Judy Beauchamp was delegated, somewhat reluctantly, as the guinea pig and carefully strapped on
to the flimsy seat. We then lowered her gingerly out of the
window while I played the anchor role, clutching my wardrobe for extra support, so that if the rachet slipped at least the
wardrobe and I would jam in the window. To our surprise,
the system worked impeccably, but to extend the fun we
pretended that the escape pulley had stuck and left poor old
Judy dangling about forty feet off the ground, her legs swinging wildly. Unfortunately, those legs were swinging directly
in front of a set of french windows which happened to belong
to the principal's flat. The rest of the story is pretty obvious,
and once poor Judy had been released, we were all marched
into the principal's study for a lecture.

Although Dartford is essentially a physical education college, the pupils are encouraged to become involved in other
subjects. For my supplementary lectures, I had chosen speech
and drama, and the lecturer soon discovered that she was in
for a troublesome time. It may surprise people to know that

I have my self-conscious moments – but it certainly showed through in my attempts at acting, and particularly dancing. I could never take country dancing seriously, with all that 'Take your partners, up the floor and bash her head against the door' stuff, and I've no doubt my scepticism showed through in class. During one lesson in which I'd been fooling about, our lecturer called me up to the front and demanded to know my name. 'Heyhoe,' I replied. 'I said I want to know your name,' she repeated, to which my only reply was 'Heyhoe.' This went on for some time, until she quite naturally lost patience and ordered me out of the room. It wasn't until I returned at the end of the lecture, complete with name tabs off my clothes, that she realised I hadn't been as facetious as she thought.

Modern educational dance, as it was called, left me equally cold. This involves one in exaggerated artistic and expressive ballet-type movements and one is supposed to concentrate the mind on deep, therapeutic thoughts. It was all beyond me and my lack of application led eventually to my being suspended from the class because I was a 'disturbing influence!'.

Most people tend to remember their college days as much for the social life as anything else, and I am no exception. We were close enough to London to make regular weekend excursions into the West End, and many of us became great theatre-goers.

This was the era of *At The Drop of A Hat*, *Salad Days*, *West Side Story*, and my own special favourite *My Fair Lady*, which was showing at Drury Lane, a theatre where we had our private, strictly unofficial back entrance. We had discovered that by waiting until the end of the first act, it was possible to slip in through a fire exit and take a free seat for the remainder of the show. This plan was put into operation whenever we couldn't get into another show of our choice, and I ended up seeing two-thirds of *My Fair Lady* seven times. It starred Rex Harrison and Julie Andrews and its music is still among my favourite.

Being an all-female establishment, our college was obviously much in demand for social functions at the nearby military training schools, and we became a sort of amateur escort agency when the passing-out balls came around at Gillingham Army Officer Training School and Greenwich Royal Naval College. (The latter took place in the magnificent Painted Hall at the Naval College.)

The serious business, however, was the sport, and luck followed me again in the provision of Mary Duggan and Ruth Westbrook on our teaching staff. Mary was then the captain of the England women's cricket team and Ruth, who later married cricketer Roger Prideaux of Northants, Sussex and England, was the national wicketkeeper. It goes without saying that both were major influences as I graduated to cricket captain of the college.

I also played in the first elevens at both hockey and lacrosse, despite having known nothing whatever about lacrosse when I began the course. One of the ironies was that Mary Pilling, later to succeed me as England cricket captain, was a team-mate in our college cricket, lacrosse and hockey elevens.

A year from the end of my spell at college, I was selected for my first overseas cricket tour. That probably sounds exaggeratedly grand, because the tour was only a four-day affair to Holland with a Women's Cricket Association squad – but it was further significant progress. Even for a short trip like this, the players had to shoulder all the cost themselves and hand over the princely sum of £7 11s to cover the price of rail and ferry tickets.

We set off by rail from Liverpool Street on a Friday in late July, and enjoyed a calm ferry crossing from Harwich to The Hook, followed by another train journey to Amsterdam. On the Friday evening, a welcome supper was thrown for us by the De Kieviten club in Wassenaar, and being the polite English guest I'm afraid I allowed myself to be goaded into consuming quite an amount of the fiery Dutch Bols gin.

At the age of twenty, I felt very uncertain whether I would ever reach twenty-one!

As usual on these trips, we were billeted out into private houses, and I was sharing accommodation with Audrey Winterbottom – another irony, as eighteen years later she was to be the chairman of selectors with the task of telling me that I had not been chosen as England captain for the 1978 tour of India. In Holland we got on famously, for we both shared a similar sense of humour – then!

The cricket in Holland was scarcely spectacular and played on matting wickets. That country has always ranked among the Cinderella nations with regard to cricket, and despite the fact that our team was nothing like a true representation of England's best, we won both our matches without undue concern.

After playing at tourists in the traditional way, with guided boat trips and sightseeing tours of Amsterdam, we closed the tour with a farewell dinner on the Monday evening. Some of the Dutch girls spent most of the meal trying to teach me their language, and a perfect opportunity to test my skill arose when, of all things, a fly landed in my wine. Prompted by the Dutch, I rehearsed their equivalent of 'Waiter, I've got a fly in my wine' time after time. Then, smug that I was in impressive control of the phrase, I summoned the nearest waiter and told him: *'Ober, er is een vlieg in mijn wijn!'* It had been a perfect effort and I felt quite proud until he replied in deep but faultless English: 'Have you really, madam? Let me remove it for you.'

The boat trip home was appallingly rough. It was a scheduled six-hour crossing but it took nearer eight as we headed north towards Newcastle in search of calmer waters, before following the east coast down to Harwich. Ninety per cent of the passengers must have been seasick, but I was grimly determined not to succumb. Plied with boiled sweets by Audrey Winterbottom, I simply clung on to the rail and fixed my stare on the lurching horizon. I didn't move from that position throughout the eight hours, but I made it back on to dry land without being sick.

The final year at Dartford was a slog, with the constant thought that I had to get through the exams at the end of it if I was to fulfil my ambition and become a teacher. I think my willpower might have let me down if I hadn't received a letter early in 1960, telling me that I had been chosen to go on England's four-month cricket tour of South Africa, due to begin in October. That news gave me impetus and incentive to work through the year. I passed my finals and for my first job I taught PE at Wolverhampton Municipal School for the seven weeks that remained before departure for South Africa.

It hadn't really been as straightforward as that, of course. Nothing ever is. For, with the letter inviting me to be one of the touring party, the small print made reference to a little matter of cost. Each girl in the team was expected to pay her own way to South Africa and back – £250 for the honour of representing her country. This was my first real confrontation with the sad facts of life a woman cricketer has to put up with, and for a time I wondered if I would even be able to go. Even today, £250 is a lot of money for a girl just out of college to find. In 1960, it was a fortune, and I could not have managed it without the marvellous support of my parents, who willingly sacrificed the new car they had been planning to buy in order to ensure my passage to South Africa.

On 27 October 1960, I left England for the tour which I still believe to be the most memorable I have ever been on, partly because it was my first but chiefly because South Africa, apartheid apart, is such a wonderful country for a visitor.

The Women's Cricket Association, insisting on the Victorian image, told each of us we must wear a hat on departure day, and I still have the team group photograph which appeared in *The Times*, my hat looking just what it was – a jumble-sale bargain!

Above: 10 Spot the deliberate mistake! Twenty-four variable forward defensive strokes being coached by RHF and Anne Sanders in Melbourne, 1970. *Below:* 11 The first-ever women's touring cricket team in Jamaica, 1970. English girls pose at Sabina Park, Kingston, with (front row, second and fourth left) Sue Hayward and her patron father Jack, plus Jamaican coach Derief Taylor from Warwickshire County Cricket Club

Above left: 12 Mike Smith (left), Warwickshire and England cricket captain with (right) Billy Wright, my Wolves and England football hero and now head of sport with ATV, posing with two dummies at the opening of a Wolverhampton sports shop. *Above right:* 13 'British Airways takes care of you' – and so does Jack Hayward! Pictured with Jack, our mascot, as we arrive in Freeport, Bahamas, at the start of a magical mystery tour in 1971. *Below:* 14 The 1971 England women's cricket team, dressed by courtesy of St Michael, with the Governor of Bermuda

Telegrams and bouquets made it an emotional farewell before we sailed from Southampton on the SS *Pretoria Castle*. The voyage to Cape Town took a fortnight and was, in itself, an unforgettable part of the tour.

At first we were regarded with curiosity, almost suspicion, by the other passengers who, we later discovered, had picked up a rumour that the WCA badges we wore stood for Women's Christian Association. When our true identity was known, the social life rapidly accelerated. Although we were travelling tourist class, we had a guaranteed passport to the first-class section because we played regular matches of deck cricket against the ship's officers. We were, apparently, the first team ever to beat the officers at this novel form of the game, and one first-class passenger, a widower, was so impressed by us that he insisted on buying us champagne after every game. Our fixtures consequently became far more regular.

The most irksome part of the journey was the morning training session. We all had to report on the boat deck at eight o'clock, before breakfast, for physical exercises and catching and throwing practice. Strangely, most of the tennis balls we had brought for practice purposes disappeared over the side of the ship rather rapidly!

A party was given on our last night on board, lasting long into the early hours. At four in the morning, the entire team appeared on deck, straining to catch the first glimpse of Cape Town. Quite suddenly, the sun peeped over Table Mountain, throwing an eerie, palest pink suffused light on to the white splashes of waves breaking on the shore. It was one of the most breathtaking sights I have ever seen.

Although sorry to leave the friends (particularly boyfriends) we had found on the ship, we were by then keen to get ashore, see the country and begin the real business of the tour. During the ten weeks which followed, we played thirteen matches without being beaten. We won eight games and drew five, and clinched the four-Test series with a victory

c

at Durban, thanks chiefly to a century from our captain, Helen Sharp, who was honoured by being allowed to plant a tree to mark her historic innings.

I scored a half-century in the Johannesburg Test, but my most immodest achievement was a century in ninety-one minutes against a Southern Transvaal XI. That whirlwind innings was no doubt spurred by the presence in the crowd of Clive Hornby, a boy I had met on the ship and was determined to impress!

If I had any illusions about my ability, however, I was brought heavily to earth in the final Test at Cape Town. The *Pretoria Castle* had docked, ready to ship us back to England, and the officers, most of whom we had got to know pretty well on the outward journey, all came to watch the game on the very beautiful Newlands Test Ground.

As I walked out to bat, rather over-full with confidence, the outcoming batsman, Ruth Westbrook, warned me to keep a close watch on the short-leg fielder, who was crouching only a few feet from the bat. I did – I watched her so well that I played my first ball straight into her hands and had to make the long walk back to the pavilion, head hung low, after a most inglorious duck.

Several thousand people turned up to watch us at Cape Town, many more than we would ever expect for a match in England then, and although we won the series, we came away impressed by the standard of women's cricket in South Africa. Sadly, though, they have not developed since then after being virtually ostracised from international sport by their apartheid policies.

We had been warned early in the tour to make absolutely no comment on the racial issues of the country, but it was, naturally, impossible to complete a tour without noticing them. I found it strange and sad, but retained the view that it was their country, and hardly the place of any English people to criticise. The situation worked in our favour in an odd way, as we found ourselves widely supported by the coloured population, who no doubt saw us as the opponents of their oppressors.

Eric Rowan, a Springbok Test player, was chairman of the South African women's selectors and had obviously lent his experience to great effect. I am sure many of our top officials in England might frown upon the idea of having a man in charge of team selection, but I believe the benefits would be enormous.

Socially, the tour could hardly have been bettered. Functions were arranged for us everywhere we went, and in Port Elizabeth the officials were so concerned that we should have male escorts for a dinner-dance they had laid on that they advertised for them in the local paper! All fifteen of us were fixed up with 'blind dates' but we agreed that there would be fifteen Cinderellas leaving the ball together at midnight – fifteen men wanted for fifteen sporty women for the night was too much of a risk!

The only time I felt homesick was, predictably, on Christmas Day. We came off the beach at Durban and sat with watery eyes while the Queen's speech was relayed from England on the radio.

Generally, however, it was an experience that only intensified my desire to become a regular tourist. The weather, the cricket and the life all suited me perfectly, and the most difficult part of it all was trying to re-adjust to a mundane life back in England. This, more than anything else, was to have a disruptive effect on my teaching career. I toyed with the idea of going back to South Africa to live, but had enough sense to realise that there is a great contrast between being an honoured visitor and a resident. So I stayed in England, wondering with increasing regularity whether teaching was really the life for me. I even went so far as to resign my post at the Municipal Grammar School with the intention of accepting an offer from a sports company. When they let me down, though, my father persuaded me to give teaching another chance, and I became head of PE at a bi-lateral

school called Northicote on the tougher side of Wolverhampton.

Many of the pupils at my new school came from deprived
families and difficult backgrounds, but I grew to enjoy their
rebellious nature and understand their attitudes and even their
ripe language. As a supporting subject, I taught elementary
physiology to the first-years. I suppose it was inevitable really
that one day, while I was lecturing about the birds and bees,
frogs, rabbits and butterflies, one bright little Herbert would
put up his hand and ask: 'Where do babies come from,
miss?' I promised a full explanation in our next lesson and
spent the week preparing my first-ever sex lesson. All went
well and I was drawing towards the end, feeling quite proud
about my teaching on adolescence, when a particularly wicked
boy in the back row interrupted: 'Please miss, can you tell
me when I will be ready?'

By now, my first vehicle had been abandoned and I'd
graduated to four wheels. The Vespa scooter that had carried
me around for some time had finally become just too difficult. Travelling to social functions on it had become a joke,
as I would invariably arrive with my pencil-thin skirt rumpled
or torn and my new hair-do looking like a bush in a storm.

It had given me one or two painful experiences, too,
specifically on the day in 1961 when I had ridden from
Wolverhampton to Chislehurst, in Kent, for a WCA XI
match the following day at Meopham Green.

This was a distance of 150 miles, without the help of
motorways, and I needed to stop about three times on the
way to give a few moment's rest to my aching nether regions.
When at last I reached Chislehurst, the relief was such that I
decided to finish the journey with a Barry Sheene flourish. As
I swung the scooter into the road where my friend Ann Jago
lived, the machine and I parted company. I hit the ground
with a force that was to give me a huge bruise on my right
leg, and the scooter came to rest in my arms. Ironically, I
recovered from the shock well enough to score a century

the next day. Perhaps I should try falling off a few more scooters!

My first car was a brand new Mini-van which I couldn't really afford. It was a smart, grey vehicle, which I fitted out with comfortable Axminster carpets and frequently used as a school bus for the netball or hockey team. It was a great help to me as a teacher, but I soon developed a passion for sports cars.

One night, I was flipping through the car adverts in the local paper when my eyes latched on to the car of my dreams – a red MG Midget. On impulse, I drove to the garage to look it over, and fell in love on the spot. The Mini-van was exchanged, I sank into debt and ever since then I have clung faithfully to the sports-car image.

The following year, I became heavily involved in fund-raising activities for the 1963 visit of the Australians. Many matches and functions were arranged and after one such fixture against a local men's side, I was driving home late at night in the Midget. Impatient to get back, I did some amber-gambling at a set of traffic lights, only to find a similar 'gambler' crossing my path. I hit the other vehicle – a Mini-van, ironically, driven by another woman – broadside on and lurched forward into the windscreen. I wasn't badly hurt myself, apart from cut knees, but the impact had thrown open the passenger door of the Midget, and all the money collected that evening had spilled out over the road. When the police arrived, I must have been an odd, slightly suspici-ous sight, scrambling around on all fours picking the scattered finances.

Fund-raising now became increasingly important, both to me and every other prospective England cricketer, and it wasn't long before I had my first experience of playing cricket against a top-class men's side. It came at the end of the 1963 home series against the Australians when we had won the final and deciding third Test at the Oval in the last over: a match in which Mary Duggan marked her retirement by scoring a marvellous century, and in which I became the first woman ever to hit a six in a Test – with an inelegant 'hoick' at a straight ball which landed out in cow-pasture country at long-on. Colin Cowdrey agreed to bring a team to Chislehurst to meet the England women's team. It was potentially a big money-spinner for us and Colin did not let us down. His team included Jim Laker, Len Hutton, Peter Parfitt, Peter Richardson, Peter Walker, Brian Johnston and Colin himself – and it was a tremendous day's cricket.

The men scored more than 300 before declaring, delighting in the small boundaries, but after contriving a finish by keeping us in the chase they eventually found themselves helpless to prevent a victory for the women in the final over. I had perished in the 40s, however, through my own gambling instincts. Len Hutton was standing at slip during my innings, and at the end of an over, he said he would give me £5 – a fortune from a Yorkshireman! – if I hit Jim Laker over the sightscreen. That was a challenge I couldn't refuse, and when Jim next pitched one up, I drove him fiercely, back over his head. I could almost feel the crisp fiver as the ball soared away towards the sightscreen – but I hadn't reckoned on the tallest man on the field, six-foot-five-inch Peter Walker. Running round from long-off, he took the catch high above his head, robbing me of a fiver and kicking my impulsive nature in the teeth.

This match was a prelude to my being chosen as England captain for the first time in 1966 to face the New Zealanders here at home in England. It also gave me the idea to run a Sunday women's XI against men's teams all over the country to expand our meagre funds.

When I was appointed captain against the New Zealanders I knew there was some opposition to my leading England: some officials thought I was too flippant and facetious to be a responsible captain. Feeling that I had a point to prove, I managed to score a century in the first Test at Scarborough.

The reports of our Scarborough Test were so minimal in

the national Sunday papers that I myself determined in
the future to get our sport more fully recognised. One Sunday
paper recorded our scores in two minuscule lines of type under
the bowls column. Perhaps they thought we still bowled
underarm!

6 Following on

Ask any man who has played cricket for England which caps he treasures most and he will invariably tell you about those he has won against Australia. It's no different in women's cricket – the aura of the Ashes and the lure of battles against the 'enemies' from down under outshine almost anything else the game can offer.

It needs no emphasising, then, that the England women's tour of Australia and New Zealand in 1968–9 meant a great deal to everyone picked. It also cost a great deal of money and demanded an extraordinary amount of planning – and trials for places on that tour were conducted in the summer of 1967.

Yes, it was a crazy situation. But there was little alternative. Ten of the touring party of sixteen were named and notified before the end of the 1967 season, almost eighteen months before the scheduled departure. This method, for all its disadvantages, at least gave those selected some much-needed time to raise cash. For in the customary letter from the WCA, formally inviting us to tour, we were politely informed that we would need not only twelve pairs of socks, half-a-dozen skirts and shirts and a toothbrush, but also £600!

Those were the days before major sponsorship, and the players were left very much alone to do their fund-raising. The eighteen months could be precious – but they could also be painful for anyone acutely losing form to the point where inclusion on the tour was an embarrassment to the selectors, the other players and the poor girl concerned. There was also the chance, of course, that a few new talents would emerge in the period before departure, which was why six places were left open until the following season. The system was neither foolproof nor totally approved of, but it was understandable if the financial problem was to be overcome.

So, at the close of the 1967 season, I was told that I would be going to Australia – as captain of England. I determined there and then that the team should all tour at as little personal cost as possible, and in conjunction with my vice-captain Edna Barker and Audrey Disbury – one of the England 1977 selectors – I set to work to raise funds.

We made an encouraging start by taking a side to play a men's club team in a suburb of Walsall and coming away with £100. Suitably spurred, the three of us wrote something like five hundred letters to every imaginable concern, urging, cajoling, begging them to make some kind of donation.

A personnel officer from London called Brian Lancaster, an East Grinstead club cricketer, was appointed as our fund-raising co-ordinator and his first major coup was to obtain the promise of £500 worth of clothing from Marks and Spencers, allowing the girls a number of free outfits each to supplement the tour blazer – which, believe it or not, we had had to buy ourselves. In order to cover her financial outlay for the tour, Val Hesmondhalgh, the team's manageress, taught full-time during the day and took a night-shift job on the assembly line of an instrument manufacturer. She displayed a type of dedication which is very scarce in these days of greedy professionals.

We aimed to collect a total of £11,000 for our tour, and I must say most people were very generous, either contributing cash or material needs. By the time we left, my room at home had grown to resemble a market stall, cluttered with cans of deodorant, chewing-gum, soap, toothpaste, shampoo, films, shoes, face-cream and countless other items, all sent by helpful companies.

The team travelled the country playing fund-raising matches, and I found myself out almost every night of the week, speaking to cricket clubs, social clubs and companies at their functions, to spread our gospel and cut our costs a little more. By the end of most evenings, I had the diners crying into their beer at my stories of how little financial help we were given, and the collections were incredibly generous.

I remember speaking at one particular cricket function, at a small club in Yorkshire. The men passed the hat round afterwards and presented me with £60. My appreciation of their tremendous gesture was great – what a comparison with the MCC, by whom the WCA are recognised as a constituent member of the National Cricket Association, who only found it in them to give us 150 guineas – not even three times as much as the little Yorkshire cricket club collected.

Apart from MCC's official donation, we were also given a grant by the Sports Council – vital and particularly important to us as it came from a government body. We then, however, received veiled threats that the entire grant might be withheld if we insisted on pursuing a plan to call into South Africa on our way out. Our aim had been simply to break the journey with a few days in South Africa and play a couple of warm-up matches, but the Sports Council, presumably under direction from above, told us in no uncertain terms that this was not a good idea.

I deplored this intrusion. It was the first time ever that my sporting life had run head-on into a political barrier and I didn't like it at all. I was and am a great believer in being constructive and building bridges to help troubled situations, not destroying every link in sight. If, however, the British Government consider it their duty to register their disapproval of South African policies I suggest they cut off every contact with them, including banking and trading links. For, as things stand, sport is merely being used as a political lever. Who are we, in any case, to tell the South Africans how to run their country? And if we are honest, can't we find other examples of oppression, perhaps just as odious, in the recent histories of countries such as Chile and Russia?

However, we had to do as we were told. The South Africa stop-over was off. We left London to a send-off worthy of film stars on 3 December 1968 and flew to Perth with about half-a-dozen stops *en route*, each apparently hotter than the last but unfortunately none of them in South Africa!

When we left London, the temperature had been 39°. When we arrived in Perth, twenty-seven hours later, it was almost 100°. It had been so humid at some of our refuelling stops in places like Calcutta and Bahrain that the wig I had packed in my cabin bag completely lost its set. When I put it on just before landing in Perth, proudly expecting to show off the highlights of my new purchase, it looked more like a dissipated hedgehog. The team loved it, of course!

We quickly felt the full power of the Australian sun when we spread ourselves on Perth beach soon after arrival. I had spent an expensive two weeks before leaving England, having sun-ray treatment to acclimatise myself, but I and several of the girls were very badly burned, purely through not realising quite how strong the sun was.

We won our first state match in Perth comfortably – a match watched by Australian Test star Graham McKenzie and the ill-fated Colin Milburn – but Jill Cruwys broke her finger to provide an omen for the rest of the trip. So beset were we by injuries that we didn't have all sixteen tourists available for selection at any one point of the stay in Australia!

Christmas was spent in Adelaide, and very pleasant it was too. But everyone's thoughts were on the first Test, just two days away. It turned out to be rather an anti-climax. Australia, instantly employing the attitude that, come what may they were not going to lose, killed the game inside two days with appallingly slow batting.

We crossed to Victoria for the New Year, and it was there, in a state game, that Enid Bakewell took seven wickets. Nothing odd about that, you may say, until told that this was the first of twelve occasions on the tour that Enid took five or more wickets in an innings. She finished the trip with 118 wickets at 9.7 runs each, and also scored more than 1,000 runs. A wonderful achievement at any level of cricket.

The second Test was played in Melbourne – another draw, although we wasted a marvellous chance by dropping a vital catch just as it seemed we could enforce the follow-on. It was in Melbourne, that E. M. Wellings of the London *Evening News* watched us play and wrote glowingly about us. He said he was more proud and impressed by the spirit and appearance of the England women's team, both on and off the field, than the often slovenly approach of the MCC team in Pakistan – where one member even took drinks on to the field, wearing his slippers!

Anything THEY can do . . .!

After brief stops in Canberra and a stay in an up-country farm, we arrived at Sydney, to my mind Australia's most exciting city although I rate Perth the most attractive place, where I could quite happily live. By this stage I was beginning to feel the load that often falls on a touring captain. Endless socials and parties demand our attendance, and it is always the responsibility of the skipper or the manager to say a few words, or chat with the local dignitaries. I began to feel very tired, and I also contracted tonsilitis. But there was a long way to go.

For the third Test, we had been assigned to North Sydney Oval, and it began with a disaster. When I walked out to toss the coin, I found that an adjoining wicket had been saturated by the groundsman. A prompt start was impossible and play was delayed for fifteen minutes while mopping-up operations were completed – otherwise we would have had to field in Wellington boots! The groundsman, somewhat grumpily, took the attitude that we were only women and he couldn't understand why we were bothered. It is an attitude that we haven't run into too often and I can't say I was very polite to him.

The match itself threatened disaster for us. Australia, casting off most of their inhibitions, topped 200 by five o'clock on the first afternoon, and our reply immediately lost its lynchpin, Enid Bakewell. I made the 'inspired' choice of Shirley Hodges as night-watchwoman, only to see her out first ball! Next morning, things went from bad to worse, and although I played a boring, anchoring 59, we were 134 for nine when Lesley Clifford and Mary Pilling came together for a salvaging stand of 60. It was enough to save the match and a third draw resulted.

Barbecues and receptions were thrown for us all over Australia, all highly memorable, especially in Sydney. One, however, given by the New South Wales Cricket Association, had a very unhappy ending. When we got back to the hotel, we were horrified to find that every one of our rooms had been rifled. Money, jewellery, cameras and cigarettes had been taken, and as no rooms other than ours had been touched there was more than a hint of suspicion pointing to an 'inside job', but the police were unable to uncover anything though they tried their hardest to solve the crime.

It was also in Sydney that Lynne Thomas woke up in the night to discover a shadowy figure going through her wardrobe. Showing more guts than I could have mustered, she sat up and demanded, in her very Welsh accent, to know what he was doing. His rather pitiful excuse was that he was looking for a friend of his, but a few strong words from Lynne told him he wouldn't find him in the wardrobe!

Sydney was our final stop in Australia and at the beginning of February we were due to fly on to New Zealand. We had had a fair amount of free time and many of the girls had used it for endless sightseeing trips. Not me! In that respect, I am definitely not a good tourist. I never have been one for wandering around taking snapshots of ruins and scenery, either in this country or abroad, and I tended to spend most of my spare time following my own favourite pastime of sunbathing.

On our last full day in Australia, however, it suddenly occurred to me that I hadn't seen a single koala bear. Even I couldn't leave Australia without that experience, so the next day I got up early and cheated, taking my camera down to Sydney Zoo to film the furry friends standing inside their compound so that I could pretend I was really out in the wilds!

New Zealand was visibly a different proposition from the moment we landed in Auckland. Not having seen a drop of rain for two months, we were rather surprised to find that, in a country so close, the weather was damp at best, and frequently very soggy! It spoiled the first Test at Wellington when both teams had scored more than 300 in their first innings. At the Basin Reserve Test ground in Wellington, Trish McKelvey, the home captain, scored 155, which was the highest score for New Zealand by anyone, male or female.

While in Wellington, we stayed in a Salvation Army-run hotel – with no smoking in the dining-room and no alcoholic drinks allowed on the premises – which trimmed our wings a little. We did smuggle some drinks in but little did we realise that we probably had every secret sip monitored! One day I was just leaving my room to go out when the intercom called: 'Telephone call for Miss Heyhoe.' Because I was late I shouted ahead to some of the other girls, 'Where the hell is the damned phone?' and the voice in the ceiling came back, 'Downstairs, Madam, in the foyer.' Shades of Big Brother, I thought!

My thoughts may not entirely have been on that Test as, just before it began, I had received a surprising letter from my boyfriend of almost a year. I had thought it odd as soon as I saw the opening: a plain 'Dear Rachael' instead of something more dramatic! It went on, 'I cannot go on deceiving you any longer. I got married last week to a girl from Manchester.' When I had recovered from the obvious shock, I accepted it, surprisingly philosophically, as one of the hazards of cricket touring. It has to be faced that a great strain can be placed on any relationship during an absence of about four months and it is certainly not just the married ones who suffer. I consoled myself with the thought that I could enjoy the social life of the tour now with a completely clear conscience!

There was certainly no shortage of social events. When we flew to South Island for a match in Otago, four of the West Indians who were concurrently touring New Zealand were at the game – Gary Sobers, Lance Gibbs, Wes Hall and Jackie Hendricks. They invited our entire team to dine with the West Indians, which we accepted of course, and a very lively occasion ensued! We were ushered on to our team bus at about two in the morning, at which point the West Indian boys were just getting the party properly started. Rum was flowing freely, the dancing was underway, and we later discovered that they went straight from the party to breakfast, and from there on to the field!

We were winning most of our country matches, but the tour had now provided four successive drawn Tests. Christchurch at last gave us the win we wanted – and gave me the thrill of leading England to a victory after seven successive draws (three in England in 1966) as captain. It was one of the most memorable Tests I have ever played, coming to a climax when we bowled New Zealand out on the last afternoon to leave ourselves 129 minutes in which to score 173. A tall order, certainly, but this was the clearest chance we had yet been given. Enid Bakewell and Audrey Disbury put on 84 for the first wicket in little more than an hour, and by then it was definitely on. I went out for a single-minded run chase and produced 37 in twenty-one minutes, including one 6, but the game seemed to be slipping away as Lynne Thomas struggled in vain for quick runs.

Eventually, showing a disregard for personal ego and statistics, she gave us hope by deliberately throwing her wicket and the final 35 runs came in a rush. We won by seven wickets with five minutes to spare, and the dressing-room scenes were unforgettable. For the final half-hour, I had felt unable to watch and I'd sat in the far corner of our room, studiously cutting my toe nails and filing my finger nails. Lynne Thomas had strummed monotonously on her ukelele and Audrey Disbury had stood with fingers and legs crossed, with her Maori mascot standing on its head. To this day I still have an inch-square piece of turf, cut from our Test-match-winning wicket in Christchurch, at the dead of night after our celebrations.

The final Test in Auckland was no less exciting, and at tea-time on the third and last day I feared I had undone the good work and thrown the game away. Knowing that New Zealand had not managed to score at a run a minute at any time on the tour, I set them a challenging target of 251 in 225 minutes. They took it up with relish, batted very capably and, with forty-five minutes left, they were only 62 short with six wickets still standing. The slide began with a catch that I honestly took by instinct more than design, and with the aid of more fine catches and magnificent fielding we collected those final six wickets for 19 runs in nineteen minutes, to win the series 2–0. This was a game that can only have improved the image of women's cricket, particularly as it was televised live around New Zealand. The national newspapers raved about it and I remember that one of New Zealand's most respected cricket writers, Donald Cameron, called it 'one of the most memorable games I have ever seen played, by men or women'.

New Zealand gave me a chance to try out a different but very vital type of tactic, in one friendly match we were playing. The game was staged at North Shore, very near to the docks. We were out fielding in this particular encounter when a row of bronzed British naval officers appeared on the boundary and gave great vocal support. So, as captain and being in charge of tactics, I immediately moved a fielder out so that she stood right among the handsome 'fellers' on the edge of the field. She knew the tactics and we all knew the tactics, and when the next wicket fell our deep fielder came running in to the cluster of players in the middle of the field and reported, 'There's a party on the ship tonight – how many want to go?' This proves that women place as much importance on tactics while touring as the men do!

We spent the rest of our stay in New Zealand making abortive attempts to sunbathe under cloudy skies, then set off on a roundabout route home on 3 April. Twenty-four hours were spent in the sweltering heat of Fiji – a suntan at last! – and we had the odd experience of enjoying Good Friday twice as we crossed the International Dateline, which must have been good for our souls!

While in Fiji we enjoyed joining in the ancient *kava* drinking ceremony at our hotel – good traditional tourist activity. We all had to sit cross-legged on the floor while the wooden drinking-bowl of *kava* was handed round and sipped gently. *Kava* is a liquid made from the pounded roots of a Polynesian shrub – it looks like pale, coffee-coloured milk of magnesia and tastes almost as bad. It is meant to have inebriating qualities, but as far as I was concerned it only caused indigestion.

I felt that it would be great if the team could see a bit more of the States than the view from the plane as we flew over *en route* for England, so through the kindness of the Northern Californian Cricket Association we were hosted for three nights in the San Francisco area, staying in sumptuous hotels, and we also played two games of cricket. The men from the association were absolutely overwhelming in their kindness and hospitality; the cricket was rather less acceptable, though, only because it was unseasonably cold for April – snow capped the hills on the horizon, the field on which we played had a luxuriant four-inch-deep growth of grass which slowed the ball down to a dead halt and we played on a rather undulating matting wicket which almost prompted me to ask for the Hoover rather than the heavy roller! It was so chilly that many of us left our tights on under our cricket shorts and two members fielded in gloves to prevent exposure!

Our final night was quite memorable, although I think one or two lost their memories as the alcoholic intake never abated! After our game, we were taken by the menfolk to an 'authentic' imitation *Bierkellar* where we cried, '*Ein, zwei, drei, vier!*' and lifted our *Steins* and 'drinked' our beer for about two hours. Then followed a quick dash back to the hotel, where we changed into our finery and rushed on to the British Consul General's for a lavish cocktail party which we finally left at 10 pm, with the dear Consul sitting down because he had quite enough of the cricketers and the gin. Finally after dinner (Italian-style with plenty of red plonk) we were plonked on the British Airways flight for New York.

We all sat back in our seats happy to recover from the exhausting previous twelve hours, but there was to be no peace for the wicked – the chief steward came up and asked whether the team would like to accept champagne with the compliments of British Airways. So the corks started popping and we popped across the States, by now about 80° proof! One team member (I've withheld her name to preserve her innocence) told me she never did remember getting off the plane in New

York! Not me, not me, before you all start pointing the accusing finger!

New York was our last stop, where we were introduced to 100,000 people in the New York Yankees' baseball stadium as the 'all-conquering British women's cricket stars'!

England seemed cold and uninviting after our travels. I slept for twenty-four hours, then woke up to drag myself back to work – to journalism, in which I now found myself appointed sports editor of the *Wolverhampton Chronicle* newspaper.

Our return from such a wonderful tour made quite an impact on the media and suddenly I was involved in a wide range of differing appearances. One of my greatest thrills was being the castaway on 'Desert Island Discs' – I feel you've almost arrived if you get the 'selectorial nod' from Roy Plomley! I think I was probably one of the more low-brow guests on the island; I could have chosen dozens of records for I have such a variety of musical preferences. In the end I narrowed the selection down to eight records which reminded me of eight phases of my life: Ray Conniff linked me with South Africa and the only record we had to play on board SS *Pretoria Castle* as we steamed home; Joyce Grenfell's 'Nursery School' reminded me of my college and teaching days; the Seekers stood for Australia; an extract from Purcell's *Dido and Aeneas* recalled our school opera; Dvorak's *New World Symphony*, my happy days in America; Maori singers, New Zealand; the Beatles, I chose because I love their music and pupils at one of my schools had queued to get tickets for me for a concert of theirs; Elgar's *Pomp and Circumstance* stood for patriotism and England, the country I like best in the world.

Roy Plomley, incidentally, is a descendant of Queen Henrietta Maria, wife of Charles I; and I was also fascinated to discover that the seventeenth- and eighteenth-century part of his family tree reveals several Heyhoe families from Norfolk, so, who knows, we not only might be related but I also might have just a drop of royal blood in me – just call me Duchess Flint!

7 Hayward

If I hadn't been so boringly persistent in the fund-raising field, I would probably never have met Jack Hayward – and without him women's cricket would certainly not have made the strides it did during the seventies.

It all happened quite by luck really. On returning from the '68–69 tour of Australia and New Zealand, I'd been surprised by the public acclaim which greeted the team, and suddenly, I found myself on the public-appearances band wagon. Dinner speaking was the most regular request, and in the interest of promoting women's cricket I accepted almost every invitation, which wasn't easy. I was committed to three or four speaking engagements most weeks. Each one gave me a renewed sense of pleasure, because it at least meant that women's cricket was finally beginning to gain public acceptance in England.

During daytime hours, I was enjoying my job as the sports editor of the *Wolverhampton Chronicle* and making sufficient headway to create a difficult personal decision when I received a letter from Australia inviting me to go back as a coach in the coming November. If I had had any pressing family responsibilities, I would probably have rejected the offer, but my roots had not dropped and I still possessed a restless sense of ambition, so I wrote back and accepted, having obtained leave of absence from my paper.

My letter to Australia was scarcely posted when I received yet another offer via Warwickshire County Cricket Club. This time, it was to take an English team to Jamaica, early in 1970. At first we referred the invitation directly to the Women's Cricket Association, but when they refused to take it up on the grounds that the expense, so soon after the Australian tour, was prohibitive, I decided to do things myself together with Con Holden, a Midland cricket official. The tour was scheduled to last three weeks, and the cost to each player would be around £200. It was going to be very hard for the girls who had toured Australia, both to raise more money so quickly and to persuade their various bosses to give them more time off.

Money, however, was the chief obstacle, and I was discussing fund-raising ideas with some girls in our newspaper's library when one of them came up with the scheme that was to have such a far-reaching influence on women's cricket. Why, she asked, didn't I write to Charles Hayward, a millionaire industrialist, Wolverhampton-born but then based in London, and ask him for some sort of assistance? Some may have thought the idea a little cheeky, but I have the philosophy that if you never ask you never get, so my letter was in the post the same day!

When the reply arrived, a couple of weeks later, my first glance brought only a sense of disappointment. It was written by Charles Hayward's secretary and it began by apologising. Mr Hayward, it explained, was not able to provide funds for the venture. There was, however, a very significant 'but' . . .

Jack Hayward, son of the company chairman, had apparently just completed a brief visit to England from his home in the Bahamas. While in London, he had seen my pleading note and, being a cricket fanatic, had expressed an interest and a keenness to help. The upshot of it all was a suggestion from the Haywards' secretary that I should write to Jack in the Bahamas, with full details of the proposed tour. So I rushed to my typewriter and the steam flew out of it as I rattled off a hopeful letter.

Some little time elapsed after that, and with no sign of any response, I began to despair. Then one cold November evening I answered the phone at home and was asked to hold on for a call from Freeport, Grand Bahama Island. I nearly dropped the receiver, and had to sit down on the nearest chair because my legs had gone rather wobbly!

Jack Hayward came on the line like a pal from down the road, joking, chatting and enquiring about the Wolves and the weather. Then he got down to business and asked how much money we needed. Drawing a deep breath, I told him that the complete cost of the tour was £1,580. Jack Hayward merely replied, 'That's all right, I'll back the tour.'

I thought at first I had misheard or misunderstood when he said that he would pay, but I hadn't. There was nothing I could really say, and my stumbling 'thank you' must have sounded absurdly inadequate. I felt like Cinderella when the Fairy Godmother told her she would go to the ball!

Jack had apparently been following the progress of the England team for some time, and he told me he had been proud of our efforts for the Australian tour, both in raising the cash and creating a good impression out there. This, he said, was his token of appreciation.

When I eventually put the phone down I still couldn't believe what had happened. Here was someone offering to pay for our tour out of the kindness of his heart. I was alone at home and suddenly I took off and ran all over the house jumping on chairs and bouncing on beds.

We had made arrangements to meet in London the following week, when Jack was making another of his flying visits to England. I arrived at his office in St James's at the appointed time, travelling by taxi to create the right impression. Nerves jangling, I was shown in by the commissionaire and made my way up the highly polished stairs leading from the delightful panelled hallway of his London Regency town house.

I'm not sure why, but I somehow expected Jack to be different from anyone else. Certainly, though, I was anticipating nothing like the man who bounded downstairs, to shake hands with me. It was simply that he was so very normal!

At least, I thought, lunch was bound to have a special touch about it. How wrong could I be! Jack immediately whisked me into his office, where a leather-covered table in the centre of the room was laid for the meal. On a white table-cloth was a bowl of fruit, cheese and biscuits, a bowl of pickled onions and two bottles of Double Diamond! Only then did I get it into my head that Jack Hayward wanted to be nothing more than a normal Englishman, doing things that most Englishmen do – and that included eating a simple lunch.

When lunch was over, he wrote out the cheque, and even added to the required sum 'to give the girls a little spending money'. Then he picked up the phone, called his wife in his Sussex home and asked me to speak to her. The cheque-book stub revealing that he had paid the best part of £2,000 to an English girl called Rachael might, he explained, with a wicked grin, be misunderstood by his wife. So there I was, standing in the first-floor office in St James's clutching a cheque that would take fifteen girls to Jamaica and explaining to a woman I had never met before that it was all strictly above board! Jean Hayward is as kind and natural as her husband, and the events of that day were the forerunner to a lasting friendship which has since extended to several holidays and 'rest-cures' at their homes in England and the Bahamas.

I never had any suspicions about this remarkable act of philanthropy, but there are very few people in the world who hand out that sort of money to someone they have never met before and want nothing in return. Having met Jack Hayward for the first time, though, I realised he was one of the few. He wanted nothing more than the genuine satisfaction of knowing that he had helped a worthy cause and, moreover, a British one.

Jack Hayward is an avid Anglophile. Although he has in effect been domiciled abroad for the last quarter of a century, I have yet to meet a more fanatical Briton. When I first knew him, he always kept his watch on UK time, wherever he was in the world, which might explain why he was often late for appointments!

Years ago, he went to the Bahamas and set up the Grand Bahama Development Corporation, which has turned a neglected and unproductive island into a flourishing concern. Yet in all his business dealings out there, he still insists on a few English touches. The town of Freeport is a constant reminder of England with its red pillar-boxes, English pubs and English road names.

At five o'clock every day Jack will sit down with a cup of tea, because he believes Englishmen are drinking tea at that time all over the 'British Empire'. He listens to every sports report by the BBC World Service. And, perhaps even more strikingly, he will drive nothing but British cars: a notice at the gateway to his Sussex home reads, 'FOREIGN CARS PROHIBITED'.

Jack once spent £150,000 on buying Lundy Island for the National Trust to save it from the inevitable commercial development. In a similar cause, he spent another £150,000 on the damaged SS *Great Britain* (Brunel's first iron ship) and had it towed back to England for renovation. *Private Eye* once referred to Jack as 'the eccentric millionaire who has saved such ancient British relics as Lundy Island, SS *Great Britain* and the England Women's Cricket Team'. All I can say is that I'm glad I've survived as a relic.

Jack's love of England is so acute that he has earned the nickname 'Union Jack', and it seems rather ironic that the lengths of his visits to the country he loves are now limited.

He admits that there are many things about England which he misses, primarily Wimbledon, Royal Ascot, the Test matches, the countryside and British beer. But he has compensated, in part, by exporting various parts of England to his home on Grand Bahama Island. A London taxi was one of the first items to be shipped over, as well as an ancient Rolls-Royce. London red double-decker buses have followed – in fact almost everything British except the *Queen Mary* and London Bridge!

More recently, Jack has had four racing yachts built for

round-the-world yachtsman Chay Blyth, predictably called *GB I, GB II, GB III* and *GB IV*, and in 1977 he donated £75,000 – half the total cost – to the building of the new indoor cricket school at Lord's, now fittingly named after him.

So there I was in 1970, walking on air out of Jack's office with enough money to complete the tour of Jamaica at no cost to the players, which was more than I had ever dared hope for. I was by now, of course, fairly persistent with issuing press releases, and Jack Hayward's donation gave me another chance to publicise the advances of women's cricket. Newspapers seized on the story and the tour took on a great novelty value. When the team flew off from London, most people in England who read the sports pages or the social gossip pages knew where and how they were going.

They flew without Anne Sanders and me, however, for we had been in Australia for six weeks, carrying out our coaching contract. Indeed, my exit from England, in late November, had been considerably more dramatic than the team's in January.

I first knew something was wrong at the airport, when the customs official spent what seemed a very long time staring at my passport and then at me – I thought it was my Borstal-type passport photo which appealed to him! Finally, he made the solemn announcement that my passport had expired, and I couldn't leave the country. I was stunned. After a session of pleading, he agreed to let me through his gate, but stressed that he couldn't guarantee I would be allowed on the plane – that was the decision of the airline who had the responsibility of flying me back to England if I was refused entry into Australia. The worst happened and I was stopped from boarding: the duty officer told me I could not travel without a valid passport, and that appeared to be that. By then, I was in tears, as much at my own stupidity as anything else, but I was saved by the fact that I had a paid return ticket, which released British Airways from any liability in the event of my not being allowed into Australia. While all this had been going on, our plane had been delayed for thirty minutes – purely on my behalf – and the icy stares that greeted my eventual arrival in the cabin said more than any words could have done.

The coaching course went much as planned, and for the second year in succession, I spent Christmas in the heat of Australia. This time, I spent Boxing Day at the Melbourne Cricket Ground and experienced Test match-watching in a bikini for the first time in my life. I must say I preferred it to the winter woollies and rugs so often necessary in England!

When our duties were over, Anne and I spent three days on Palm Beach in Florida, where an airline contact of mine had negotiated free hotel accommodation for us. But although we paid nothing for the rooms, we were still staggered by the expense of food and drink. Beer was the equivalent of £2 per can, so if we felt thirsty and rich we would share one! A sun-chair next to the swimming pool was about the same price, so we sat on the hard concrete. For food, we slipped out of the hotel and lived on pancakes and maple syrup from a parlour round the corner.

We arrived in Jamaica three hours before the main body of the team, and were greeted in sensational style in the airport building. High above the concourse was a huge board on which lights flashed the message: 'KINGSTON, JAMAICA WELCOMES RACHAEL HEYHOE AND HER ENGLISH WOMEN'S CRICKET TEAM'. It was a superb gesture, and indicative of all that we were to find on our three-week Magical Mystery Tour.

I call it that because of the magical nature of the island and the mystery created by our being the first English women's team ever to tour there. As far as the cricket was concerned, we played three games against club sides and three two-day internationals, two of them at the famous Sabina Park Test ground. As far as the social side of the tour was concerned, we managed to attend nineteen parties in twenty-one nights on the island!

The enthusiasm for the cricket was quite stunning. More than a thousand spectators watched our games against club teams, and the final international at Sabina Park drew crowds of six thousand on each day. For me as captain, it was a particularly fascinating experience. A captain expects some advice from her team-mates every now and again, but in Jamaica, I received constant vocal advice from the 'experts' in the crowd. Often, hanging from the trees in extraordinary positions, they would yell at me to change the bowling or the field placing, and I may even have been influenced at times in order to keep the crowd happy.

The spectators made a constant noise throughout every playing day, with their non-stop babble of conversation and clanking cans. Once, when we had taken three wickets in an innings very quickly, they began to chant passionately and for a while I was really scared that they were about to riot. When one fan rushed on to the field and headed straight for me, I thought my number was up! Instead, in a charming little ceremony, he presented me with a toilet roll and galloped off into the trees again. At least he was more polite than our senseless football 'fans' who hurl their Andrex rolls all over the goalkeeper.

After one of the internationals, we had to travel by car up to the north shore for a club match. The journey took a seemingly endless seven hours, due to a number of punctures and breakdowns among our convoy. It was frustrating enough to be held up for so long, but during one puncture interlude I completely lost my temper when a car-load of West Indian lads went past, the passengers jeering loudly at our misfortune. I happened to be standing by the side of our car finishing an apple, and in a moment of rash anger, I hurled the apple core at the passing car. I'm sure I could never do it again if I tried, but the core went straight through the car's open window and smacked one of the lads on the ear! Fortunately our Jamaican hosts calmed down the lads who reversed angrily and stormed over to sort me out!

We came through the tour unbeaten, but the Jamaican girls were surprisingly good. They possessed many of the qualities of the West Indian men, particularly in the field, where many of them could throw full-toss into the wicket-keeper's gloves from a boundary 75 yards from the bat. The 'Tests' were all drawn, however, and I was left with the impression that, on such perfect batting wickets of baked clay, two days was simply not enough to achieve a definite result. We came closest to a win in the third game, when we failed to take the final three Jamaica wickets in the last fifty minutes of the match. Perhaps our performance in that game was inspired by the presence of our benefactor, Jack Hayward, who had flown in with his nineteen-year-old daughter Susan, to watch us play.

I think every girl in the team wanted to do well to demonstrate that we were not wasting his generosity, and we would dearly have loved to win. Jack didn't seem to mind, though. He came along to the farewell supper which the Jamaican Women's Cricket Association threw for us, and sat and listened while their representative announced that the tour had been such a huge success that they would like to invite the full, official England team back the following winter for a tour that should include three three-day Tests. Jack stood up as if he had been awaiting his cue. I suppose by then I shouldn't have been surprised by what he said, but I was. I was amazed. He looked round and told the gathering of English and Jamaican players that if they all wanted the tour next year, he would provide the money for England to come out!

My one disappointment on the tour was that I never met one of the women cricketers referred to in an article on West Indies cricket in the *Sunday Times* colour supplement which I had read a few months before we made the trip; one male coach of one of the women's teams in Jamaica was quoted as saying: 'No woman in England would dare face up to Mabel, our fast bowler, because, man, when she bowls everything swings but the cricket ball!'

8 Caribbean

Jack Hayward's next cricket enterprise was to involve not just Jamaica, but also other cricket-playing islands in the Caribbean, with his 'own' island in the Bahamas the idyllic starting-point. He initiated the Hayward Trophy, to be played for between Jamaica, Trinidad and England, and took such care over all arrangements that one could have mistaken him for a life-long devotee of women's cricket.

We were not due to leave until the New Year of 1971, however, and the intermediate summer was a far from idle one. Quite apart from the expansion of my journalism career, the volume of cricket commitments was in no way decreasing. It was, however, becoming more diverse, and 1970 provided me with some matches to cherish.

One of the most amusing and memorable was held in the grounds of a Surrey country house on the eve of Royal Ascot. It was between the wives of the horse owners and trainers and a team of racing journalists. I was 'smuggled' in to play for the wives – a brainchild of Colonel and Mrs Tom Wallis, who entertained me at their house in Camberley together with owners Dana and Paddy Brudenell Bruce (daughter and son-in-law of Stanhope Joel, the late famous owner).

If for nothing else, this game was remarkable for the fact that it was played on a pitch the size of a rather square tennis court. Boundaries came more easily than usual, and I actually won the match for the wives with a straight six into the cabbage-patch, with *Telegraph* racing correspondent Lord Oaksey peering through an intervening hedge!

The whole occasion was warm and hospitable, but I would have accepted the invitation if only for the opportunity to go to the Ascot meeting, which I found a completely delightful,

traditional day out. Being something of a sentimentalist, I
must admit it left a lump in my throat, when the Royal
Family made their drive down the course.

If Ascot is one of the great English traditions, Wimbledon
is certainly another, and I was lucky enough to have a similarly
unusual involvement in this, too. Journalists seem to enjoy a
game of cricket, whatever their working sport may be, and
this time I was drafted in to play for the tennis writers against
the stars of Wimbledon.

Midway through our innings, one of the fielding side could
be seen lying on his back sunbathing in the outfield, licking
an iced lolly – and of course it had to be Ilie Nastase! He
claimed that he had never played or seen cricket before, and
the fielding session had left him so bored that he went off in
search of refreshment. He did not, however, completely cut
himself off from the game – as I found to my cost . . .

I batted with Jim Laker for quite a time, and should have
grown accustomed to Jim's dislike of the quick single. I didn't
learn, though, and when I called and set off for a quick one to
mid-wicket, Jim sent me back in a polite but unmistakeably
firm voice. I never made it, for Nastase leapt to his feet, rushed
in with the ball and broke the stumps with a great whoop of
delight.

Our women's teams were by now playing against more and
more men's teams, and we didn't always escape lightly. I
remember one particular occasion when Jack Bond, who was
then captain of Lancashire, phoned me up to ask me if I would
bring a team up to play for his benefit at Old Trafford. I
readily agreed and gathered together one of the strongest
elevens I could muster, virtually our full England side.

When we got to Manchester, though, we found that the
opposition was provided by the collective talents of the Lancashire first eleven, Clive Lloyd, Peter Lever, Barry Wood and
all. From the start, it was a huge embarrassment. Barry Wood
and Ken Snellgrove opened Lancashire's innings and each
reached 50 in no time at all. They then had a mid-wicket

chat and entered into a six-hitting competition between themselves to see who would get into three figures first. Harsh treatment it may have been, but then I see no reason why they should have been expected to spare our blushes – and it did at least stall any complacency that may have been growing in our ranks by underlining the enormous difference between top men's cricket and the best women cricketers.

Jack Hayward was in England in 1971 to watch the final trial at Hastings before the team to tour the West Indies was announced. After the selection meeting, he asked me if there were any disappointments. I told him that selection had omitted Anne Sanders, who had been an integral and popular part of the previous year's Jamaica tour, and Jack, who had become a great fan of Anne, spontaneously offered to pay for her to come out in the invented position of assistant manager. Just one more example of the extraordinary generosity of the man.

In that trial game at Hastings in 1970, I encountered a problem which I know the England men's captain will never have to solve in *his* career. Enid Bakewell, the Nottinghamshire mother and cricketer (in that order!) was due to open the innings for my side. She had with her at the trial her two-month-old son, and she was relieved that the lunch-time feed fitted in with our luncheon interval. But I wasn't relieved when Enid came up to me with a worried look on her face to tell me that little *enfant terrible* had wind and couldn't get off to sleep and could I possibly drop her down the batting order until the burrp had been orchestrated! It's just another facet of cricket for a captain to understand – not only the wind out on the field which governs who bowls at which end, but also the paediatric wind in the pavilion which decides who bats at what number!

Our West Indies tour did not begin without one major tragedy. On a rainy November night in London, one of the touring party, Jean Clark, lost control of her car, hit a bollard, received severe head injuries and went into a coma. She died a week later and we lost a delightful player of just 4 feet 11 inches in height but an enormous character.

We were able to spend Christmas at home, which, for me at least, was a pleasant change, and we flew to the Bahamas in early January. As expected, we were royally looked after by the Haywards, who had organised cricket, squash, hockey and hectic rounds of socialising for us, and by the time we flew on to Jamaica, the team were in exactly the right spirits.

The first Test did nothing for our humour. It was a horrible draw, with Jamaica batting second and aiming for nothing but safety. Consequently, we changed policy in the second Test and when I won the toss, I put them in to bat. Batting first, they seemed unable to judge the pace of their innings, and we hustled them out for a paltry 86. I scored an unbeaten 107 as we almost trebled their total with only two wickets down, declaring 142 ahead. We bowled out Jamaica for the second time in the match at 5.22 p.m. on the final day. Their total was 144, just two runs ahead, but with only eight minutes playing time still available, we were not allowed to start our innings. We had needed only three runs to win, and here the frustration of being so near and yet so far from victory made me readily lose my temper with both the opposition and the Jamaican administrators.

If the game had been conducted normally throughout we could have had no complaints other than bemoaning our own ill luck in coming so close. But the cause of my anger was the persistent delays, through the apparent reluctance of the Jamaicans to take the field on time. I couldn't remember a single occasion when they had been on the field promptly after an interval of any kind. Once, even the umpires had joined the farce by taking the field without the match ball and having to return to the pavilion to retrieve it! The scorebook revealed that a total of thirty-seven minutes had been lost – and if that had not been sufficient for us to score three runs then we wouldn't have deserved victory! I registered an official protest

15 The one with the handbag is our twelfth man in drag! Actually it's John Bromley, executive director of London Weekend Television's 'World of Sport', with his team in 1971. Spot Dickie Davies, Brian Moore, Derek Ufton, Neil Durden-Smith and Mickey Bear

16 Bats in the belfry! Leaving church under a Gray-Nicolls archway after our nuptials, November 1971

Above: 17 To coin a royal phrase – 'my husband and I' at Buckingham Palace with my mother, Roma Heyhoe, and my MBE, given for a Mighty Big Effort for women's cricket. *Below:* 18 Princess Anne, Jackie Stewart, Ann Moore and directors of the *Daily Express* laughing at the rattle of a simple woman revealing all about her coconut shells at the newspaper's Sportsman of the Year lunch, 1972

Above: 19 Doing a promotion for Mars Four Square Food Division with (left to right) director Chris Lawson, David Hemery, Peter Oosterhuis and ITV's Brian Moore in 1973. Watch the space for Gordon Banks. *Below:* 20 'My cup overfloweth' – Jack Hayward, sponsor of women's cricket, pours the champagne to celebrate England winning his World Cup, 1973

Above: 21 Dynamic Duo: RHF and Neil Durden-Smith poised for commentary at the Wembley women's hockey international, 1973. *Below:* 22 The 'Flintstones' at home in 1978. Hazel (20), Benjamin (3½), Rowan (15) and Simon(21)

with the Jamaican manager and with the umpires but, naturally enough, it came to nothing.

Our complaints did not end there. We were also disgruntled over the home authorities' failure to arrange any matches for us between the Tests. Whether or not this was a deliberate ploy to leave us short of match practice I wouldn't like to say. If so, it did not completely succeed, because we made some match arrangements of our own and organised fixtures against the national army officers' team.

The victory that we really deserved arrived in the third Test, which was held in the heart of Jamaica's sugar-estate country. This time we batted after winning the toss yet again, and instructed everyone to aim for quick scoring. We declared at 234 for six after less than three and a half hours, skittled Jamaica for 80 and, following on, they managed a second innings of 165. We hit off the 12 runs needed with seventy-five minutes to spare. We won despite an injury to wicketkeeper Shirley Hodges which had meant that I had had to play in unfamiliar territory – captaining in gloves and pads from behind the stumps – and very inelegant I was as well!

The first part of the tour was now completed, a success if not without its troubles, but before we left Jamaica we had more socialising to complete. This included a reception at the British High Commission which was scheduled to finish at 7.30 p.m. but was in fact still going strong until midnight during which time the High Commissioner had sent out for Chinese take-away food to feed the team!

One of my greatest personal thrills was meeting the incomparable Pele after we had watched an exhibition football match in Kingston between his own Santos club team from Brazil and Chelsea, who were out from England on tour. After the game, a joint reception was thrown for the two football teams and ourselves at a hotel. While Pele and the Santos players mingled dutifully, I was disgusted by the behaviour of our own British team from Chelsea. Shambling into the reception room, they arranged themselves on bar

D

stools with their backs to the other guests and made no effort to talk to anyone but themselves. Their manager Dave Sexton and John Hollins were exceptions.

I am well aware that constant receptions can become a bore, but I will never condone insulting ignorance and I can never forgive or forget the one Chelsea player who 'amused' himself by persistently spitting on to the mirror at the back of the bar – wonderfully couth behaviour!

Trinidad was to be the host island for the Hayward Trophy matches, and we were scarcely encouraged by a look at our itinerary which announced that we would be staying in 'The Community Workshop'! It lived up to its image, with sparse, functional furniture and none of the comforts that we had come to expect from the intercontinental hotels of previous tours. We were woken daily, at an unearthly hour, by bells ringing the other residents to the workshop classes, or, as we came to call it, 'the workhouse'.

The competition was a disappointing one for us, because we drew both our fixtures against Jamaica and Trinidad and took only six points for first-innings lead in each case. It did not pass off without another farce, either, as on the opening morning of the tournament, confusion still reigned over the playing regulations. Many West Indian people have this remarkable philosophy on life that 'everything will be all right tomorrow' and tomorrow 'soon come'. Well, I was not prepared to accept that divine interference would put everything to rights, and I refused to take the England side on to the field against Trinidad until the officials had finalised and written out the rules!

Rain interfered with this game at the famous Queens Park Oval in Port of Spain, and when we played Jamaica in San Fernando, watched by the Haywards, we simply ran out of time.

Our enthusiasm was recharged by a brief stop in Tobago, which managed at that time to cram eleven women's cricket teams on to an island the size of the Isle of Wight. This

was the Caribbean we people dream of, with lines of palm trees bowing gently on to beaches of pure white sand. Unbelievable!

Back in Trinidad, we experienced the unforgettable annual carnival, held on a scale that cannot fully be explained in words. The whole island stops completely for three days' exhausting festivities. Everyone dresses up in incredibly elaborate costumes that cost the earth and the steel bands play at street parties which go on without a break for the seventy-two hour duration. The rum consumption is pretty high and the roadsides were littered with sleeping locals who had hit the hard stuff too hard. I saw one fellow slumped against a tree, seemingly dead to the world, with a rum bottle clutched in one hand. A steel band came thumping, stomping and crashing by and the fellow leapt to his feet and off he stumbled behind the band as though hypnotised.

I managed to enjoy the first twenty-four hours of carnival before retiring to bed with a stomach upset. For the other two days, I had to be content with just the sound in the street outside the hotel, which was rather less than the Jamaican cricketers had contented themselves with, judging by their performance against Trinidad on the day following the carnival!

This was the last of the Hayward Trophy games and if there was a definite result, the winners would take 12 points and the trophy. If it finished as a draw, the trophy would come to us. Trinidad, on paper the weakest of the three teams, put victory out of reach of the lethargic Jamaicans early in the game, and appeared to take their fight away too. Jamaica surrendered the game so feebly that many people came away with the impression that they had 'thrown it' once their own chance had gone, simply so that Trinidad and not England would take the trophy.

We nearly had to stay on in Trinidad longer than planned. Jack Hayward himself drove us to the airport, and the traffic jams were so bad that he had to drive at breakneck speed whenever possible. My stomach was still a problem and we were further held up by having to find a loo in a roadside shanty house, but we reached the airport with a few minutes to spare and flew off to complete the trip with a few days' sightseeing in Bermuda and one match against the Island eleven, arranged by the Brewer and Mulder families I had met at Ascot a year earlier.

As we returned to England from a tour that had been less of a triumph than I had hoped, I was consoled and cheered by the thought that we had at least looked like a team – both on and off the field.

Unlike a number of modern-day captains, men and women, I still consider dress and conduct to be vitally important on tour. I don't like the idea of an England team slouching around at social functions wearing jeans, tee-shirts and sandals – or even sitting down to a meal dressed like that. I would never allow any team of mine to behave with the appalling manners of Chelsea's footballers in Jamaica. They made me ashamed to be British.

It was during the following summer that I became involved with Derrick Flint, was engaged in September and married him in November, but looking back through my diary for that season, it is a wonder I found time for any thoughts of marriage. All I seemed to be doing was racing up and down the country, both with my job and with my cricket. I had only two free Sundays between May and October, and that was when Derrick, his three children and I went for a holiday to Majorca.

The change in my social life seemed to do my form no harm either. I finished the season with more than 1,600 runs at an average of just over 50, which recalled the words of one of the most famous Victorian women cricketers, Lucy Ridsdale. She was the lady who played for the White Heather Club, the first-ever women's team, and she later married the prime minister, Stanley Baldwin. Interviewed later, she admitted that she had always been nervous before batting but that when she had got engaged to Mr Baldwin she had lost all nervousness. It was in 1892, the year that she married, that she achieved an average of 62, the best of her career.

My last match of this heady summer was at Hemel Hempstead in September, when I led an England team against that of England and Yorkshire's Phil Sharpe in one of his benefit year fixtures. We batted second and came very close to beating a side that contained a number of England players. Helped by some friendly leg-breaks from Keith Fletcher and a six off Norman Graham that still gives me great pride, I passed 50 and was still batting in the last over with only a few runs wanted.

The Hemel Hempstead ground has a major road running

behind the sightscreen at one end, the end from where Richard Hutton delivered that final over. I can describe the murky conditions no better than by saying that the cars which passed by all had their headlights on. But Hutton, lost in a chauvinistic attitude that defies any women's team to beat men, hurled those six balls down at a terrifying pace. He didn't get me out but we didn't win, though I'm glad I survived to tell the story!

After a super wedding and honeymoon in Marrakesh, I returned to a quieter life in Wolverhampton. Also a sadder one, for in early November, my mother phoned to say that father, who suffered from Parkinson's disease, had fallen heavily at home and broken his femur. He had been taken into hospital, and died three months later.

To this day, I feel a sorry sense of guilt that I was not with him when he died. I had called into the hospital one morning and found him asleep, so I had left to travel to Newcastle for a day's work with Tyne-Tees Television. I stayed overnight and got a lift back to Wolverhampton the next morning, arriving back at home at lunchtime. What I didn't know was that he had died overnight.

Father's death had a profound effect on me, which I was to feel for a long time. Until then, I suppose I had never given much thought to people dying. He had always been a mentor to me, always involved in whatever I had wanted to do, and ever since his death, I feel that whatever I may have achieved has been due in no small way to his early influence.

9 Nets

Hockey first made a major intrusion into my life in 1955. I was chosen as goalkeeper for Staffordshire when I was just sixteen. Eventually I established myself in the Midlands territorial side in early 1964. True to form, my first sorties into the representative world were not without their disasters and discomforts.

My first game for the area had been at Shrewsbury, where everything had gone ridiculously right for me and the Midlands beat the West 5–1. As I was sharing the goalkeeping with Hazel Feltwell, against whom I battled with great friendly rivalry for the Midlands place for years and years, my next appearance was in our third fixture, against the North at Newcastle. That all went wrong from the start.

We travelled by rail to the north-east, and while the train was waiting at Birmingham, one of the passengers jumped out to raid the buffet for some pork pies to sustain her on the trip. I was standing in the open doorway with my right hand resting against the hinges, when the whistle blew. The frantic pork-pie hunter returned and slammed the door on my finger. Not realising what she had done, but knowing that the door had not shut, she slammed it again – on the same finger.

I spent that journey with a seering pain shooting through my hand, and hardly slept at all that night. The next morning I was taken to the local hospital, where X-rays revealed that the top two joints of my third finger had been broken by the impact. Rather than pull out of the match, I had the finger put in splints, determined to play and earn the *Croix de Guerre*!

Under the circumstances, the match went reasonably well. I kept a clean sheet and we won 2–0. In fact, the entire tournament was a triumph for the Midlands, and we reached the get-together undefeated after the final fixture against the East in Catford. Despite all that, however, I was totally unprepared for what was to come.

It was traditional that the England squad should be announced at the conclusion of the territorial series, but it had not been that which had brought me to Catford. Although I had not been selected for this match, I had travelled down with some friends to watch it, chiefly out of a sense of loyalty to the Midlands. When the England team announcement came I was in another room having a drink as the president of the England Women's Hockey Association called for silence in the packed restaurant and began to read the chosen names.

A murmur of voices saying 'Where's Rachael' brought me the news that I had been named as England goalkeeper. To say that I was stunned is an understatement. I tottered into the restaurant in an utter daze, caused an outbreak of laughter by turning left instead of right towards the stage, and finally made my way up to be presented with my England badge.

For a few moments, I was alone with my thoughts on the platform, but even as the rest of the team was announced and the stage filled with my international colleagues, I couldn't emerge from my reverie. When I finally stepped down, I couldn't have told anyone the names of any other players in that side.

My overriding emotion was one of pure, unadulterated pride. Just a year earlier, I had played my first home Test match for England. Now I was to keep goal for the England hockey team – I was told later that the honour made me the first woman ever to become a double international at cricket and hockey. I still couldn't believe what had happened and even when I woke on Sunday morning I had to rush to read the *Sunday Telegraph* sports pages just to convince myself that I hadn't been dreaming.

My first international was against Wales on a steel-works ground in Swansea where the home side held us to a draw. I was generally unimpressive, and I knew that nerves got the better of me.

Just a few weeks later, we played Scotland at Wembley – the occasion of a lifetime for every hockey international. I've already told my stories of travelling down to London with a party of schoolgirls for the annual Wembley hockey match. Now, quite suddenly, I was to be part of the centre-stage – and how the butterflies fluttered with nervous anticipation.

Whenever I am nervous, I have an irritating habit of picking at the skin around my finger nails and making a nasty clicking noise. That day at Wembley I was doing this almost incessantly in the build-up to the match. I couldn't eat the lunch that was provided for the players, and afterwards – ninety minutes before the bully-off – my clubmate and England colleague, Pam Stinchcombe, led me on a walk around Wembley. We found some friends in one of Wembley's many grandstand bars, and I confess now that I settled my nerves with a single watered-down brandy, swallowed surreptitiously!

It is hard to describe my feelings on stepping out of the tunnel at Wembley that day. The crowd of 60,000 erupted when we appeared, and when that number of high-pitched voices emit a full-throated, schoolgirl roar the impact is quite shattering. Shivers ran up and down my spine and I was all-of-a-tremble! As the Scottish pipers led us out to the cacophany of noise and the heaving mass of waving scarves, banners and flags, I felt rather like one of the Christians about to be thrown to the lions. I had never heard anything like it before! In fact one of the umpires I spoke to after the match said that such was the high pitch of the thousands of voices that when she blew the whistle she didn't even hear it herself!

The match itself was quite harrowing. After a fortnight of dry and sunny weather, rain had fallen steadily for about twenty-four hours in London, leaving Wembley's superb turf resembling a paddy field. If it had been any other hockey international, I think the conditions would have forced a cancellation.

The rain abated, however, during the opening ceremony when we were introduced to the Hon. Angus Ogilvy, whose charm, in the words of Beryl Reid's Marlene, 'sent' me! Then as the national anthem was being played the weather grew worse.

Both teams wallowed in the mire ineffectually for some time, hitting passes hopelessly short as the cloying mud held up the ball. It was the mud, in fact, which helped put Scotland ahead. I rushed from my goal to clear, only to find the ball stopping dead just inside the circle and a forward beating me to it with ease. We equalised shortly afterwards, but I again played an inglorious role as Scotland regained the lead. Sprinting off my line once more in the quagmire, I slipped and fell flat on my face. More seriously, I also fell on the ball – a cardinal sin for any hockey goalkeeper as it conceded a penalty bully, the equivalent of a penalty in soccer.

I lay in the mud, practically blowing bubbles in it. When I managed to heave myself to my feet, I looked like one of the Black and White Minstrels. 'Why did I bother to have my hair done yesterday?' I thought, as I looked up and saw the umpire striding over with a look of doom on her face. Scotland scored from the penalty bully to make it 2-1 at half-time, but fortunately my blushes were saved by two second-half goals which gave England a narrow victory.

Press reports of the game criticised my policy of coming out of my normal working area. The truth of it was that if I had stayed on my line, I could scarcely have moved at all, as my kickers were swimming under six inches of water.

After the game, during the customary tea-party for teams and officials, I was introduced to Ethlyn Davies, president of the United States Women's Hockey Association. During our chat, she mentioned that she was looking for English coaches to go to America on expenses-paid trips the following winter. Attractive though this sounded, it was a scheme that needed a lot of thought, but I was certainly very interested. I left Wembley wondering whether I could accept this exciting offer.

Our next success was a 2–1 win over Holland at Manchester, where the only shot to defeat me passed at navel height and would probably have cut me in half if I'd had time to get in its way. The goal was generously allowed by the Dutch umpire! Returning to the Home International circuit we flew to Belfast. Ireland, unexpectedly, beat us 1–0 and we were consequently relegated to third place in the table, below Scotland on goal average.

On returning to teaching, I found my mind still full of the American dream – and it was a dream for me. After a great deal of thought I agreed to go and handed in my notice at Northicote School. (This was a school of variable discipline where I once had a milk bottle thrown at me by a girl after I had suggested she should pick up her bottle-tops. Fortunately her aim was not too good and my quick reaction saved me from damage.)

I left England for the States in mid-August. To those who don't know me, it may seem surprising that I elected to spend five days on a ship, instead of taking a six-hour plane hop from London to New York. The fact is, I hate flying. It is a fear, I suppose, but I would certainly do a great deal to avoid air travel – something that was to cause problems later.

I was fortunate to have a friend to turn to as soon as we docked in the States. Pam Stinchcombe, my old England hockey friend and a one-time physiotherapist in Wolverhampton, had married an American and was living in New York, so I was able to spend the early part of my stay at her house.

My first engagement was in the Philadelphia area, coaching in one of their splendid hockey camps. This one was based at a lake side in the Poconos Mountains, surrounded by beautiful pine woods. Students and schoolchildren would come from all over the States for a week at a time, to live in log cabins and receive intensive hockey coaching, mainly from British coaches.

The Americans have employed British hockey coaches for some years now, and I can foresee a similar phenomenon occurring as in soccer where the English taught the world and if we are not careful the world will teach the English. Over the years the Americans have made great strides with their hockey and they certainly approach the game in a very professional, dedicated, though somewhat intense way.

It was during my three weeks at the Poconos Camp that the idea of writing a coaching book occurred to me. I had made copious notes on my methods and tactics during my first week, and, as I was only coaching the goalkeepers, my efforts were of some specialist value. When an American teacher asked to borrow my notes, I began to think of ways in which I could use them to my benefit. Nobody, to my knowledge, had ever written a book specifically on hockey goalkeeping and this seemed the ideal opportunity to try.

I was helped in my writing task by my hatred of flying. To the amazement of Americans, who step on a plane as if it's a London bus, I would always use the Greyhound buses or trains to travel between states during my four-month spell out there. Although it made the journey time a great deal longer, it did at least give me the opportunity to sit back and expand my goalkeeping notes into book form. When the book came out it was called *Just for Kicks*, and I've no doubt it was bought by a number of people who imagined it was about drugs. Sorry if anyone was disappointed!

There were three English hockey coaches in America that winter, each with her own region to tour. One was given the eastern seaboard and one the very desirable western seaboard, which naturally left me with the more daunting prospect of the huge central region, without a sniff of sea air until very late in the trip.

From Philadelphia, I headed north-west for Cleveland, Ohio, then on to Michigan and a spell at the state university. Next, I crossed Indiana to Chicago and coached several sessions on the banks of Lake Michigan. After a spell at

Iowa State University I undertook another massive trek to Mitchell in South Dakota – corn and cattle country – where the cows seem to outnumber human beings at times.

A session at Lincoln, in Nebraska, ended my north-western wanderings and I was then faced with travelling back again to Richmond, Virginia, south of Philadelphia on the east coast. By plane it would have taken two hours. By train, it took me two days, but I didn't begrudge a minute of it. By then, I was exhausted, both physically and mentally through the strain of almost constant talking during two months of intense coaching sessions. I enjoyed having two days quite alone in my own couchette on the train and I didn't have to talk to anybody apart from the waiter in the train's restaurant car.

My last official journey for the American association was almost as long again, taking me from Virginia through North Carolina and Georgia to my final coaching appointment in Montgomery, Alabama. This time, I travelled by Greyhound bus and had to change in Atlanta. It was midnight when we arrived there, and as I sat in the bus station waiting-room, I felt anything but comfortable. In this part of the States, bus station waiting-rooms seem to be used nightly as a haven for tramps, drunks and drop-outs, and I remember thinking that it was no place for a young English 'gel' to be sitting all alone!

A cleaner was walking round sweeping up, and as he passed a particularly filthy tramp sitting opposite me, his brush flicked and overturned a carrier bag lying at the tramp's feet. The sweeper passed on, but my eyes were drawn to the open end of the bag, and two evil beady little eyes that were peering at me from it. Bravery had no place in my feelings now; I hastily abandoned my seat and rushed to the security desk to tell the duty man of the live 'thing' in the bag. This guard was a hulking brute of a man, festooned with pistol, truncheon and handcuffs; yet even he was visibly nervous as he gingerly righted the bag and carried it outside. When he returned, I asked him what he had found. It turned out that the animal had been a possum, a rodent often caught by tramps for cooking and eating – what a delectable greasy menu!

I managed to arrange a few days' extra coaching in Jacksonville, Florida, which I intended to combine with some sunbathing and general relaxation before my return to England. Again, the Americans doubted my sanity as, although it was late November and a cool 70°, I still managed to touch up my tan in solitary confinement on the beaches.

So ended four months of coaching and more than 5,000 miles of travelling across North America. I had discovered very early in my stay the need to specify that I was a *field* hockey coach to avoid the natural confusion with ice hockey, which is far more widely played. Even then, however, field hockey was showing signs of developing, particularly in Philadelphia and New England. In the Mid-west, however, I often felt like a missionary.

In one college where I coached, the pupils were so obviously influenced by ice-hockey that they insisted on using both sides of the stick, stopping the ball with their feet – in fact, doing everything that is prohibited in field hockey. They then looked at me in open-mouthed amazement when I tried to put them right, as though I was the great white preacher.

I stayed in very few hotels, spending my few days at each place in private homes. In South Dakota, however, this provided the unexpected. The woman who was putting me up during my stay was a very amusing person. She explained on the way from the station to her house that her husband verged on alcoholism and she was forced to hide the bottles of drink. That night, she and I shared a few beers, then went to our rooms. I found it hard to get comfortable in bed, and when I investigated, I found a number of bottles of Bourbon stacked under the mattress. It was a good job I wasn't an alcoholic or I might never have seen the next morning.

The hospitality I was shown throughout my stay, however, was quite extraordinary and overwhelming. Everywhere I went, I was treated royally as the English coach 'who has come to help us'. I was wined and dined, treated to parties and receptions and generally spoiled, which was fine apart from the fact that it increased my weight by something like 1½ stone in four months!

In Jacksonville, I went into a bank to change some money and started chatting to the very friendly cashier. He asked what I was doing, and when I told him I was a hockey coach looking for a motel to spend a week's holiday, he immediately invited me to dinner with his wife and himself that night. What's more, his wife accepted that he was 'bringing an English girl home' without a qualm, cooked a marvellous meal and then sorted out a hotel for me the next day. It really couldn't happen in England, where everyone tends to be so stand-offish and shy of making conversation with strangers.

I devoted a good deal of my spare time in the States to playing ten-pin bowling, for which I developed quite a passion. I also watched a lot of baseball, which I found remarkably civilised compared to the discomforts you have to endure when you go to football matches in England. To begin with, almost all baseball stadiums are accessible by public transport, but, if you want to drive, parking space is plentiful. It's easy to reach your seat without being pushed and shoved around, and at the Philadelphia Stadium where the famous Phillies play, stewards polish every seat before the customer sits down. Food and drinks are brought round to your seats, thus avoiding the undignified scramble under the stands we have in England in order to get a tasteless cup of tea. All in all, British soccer could learn quite a few lessons from American sports – specifically, that promoting your sporting product means pampering the customers, not just getting the players on the pitch and making the supporters suffer discomfort and poor service.

I left New York in early December, on the SS *United States*, purported to be the fastest liner across the Atlantic. It certainly did achieve a speed, but it also rattled appallingly in the rough weather which we suffered. The nightly dances were amusingly affected, for as the ship lurched to and fro, the rolling and pitching sent the dancers hurtling in an involuntary stampede from one side of the floor to the other. 'Come Dancing' would be much more fun in such conditions!

On one particularly rough night, the dance was cancelled, probably to save expense as much as anything else, for the poor waiters were regularly putting trays of drinks on tables, only for a lurch of the ship to heave and smash them on to the floor.

I survived without being seasick, thanks to a cure suggested to me by a steward on my cricket trip to South Africa. Whenever it became really rough, I would drink a couple of port-and-brandies, then go up on to the deck and keep walking about, my gaze fixed on the horizon. It worked remarkably well.

We landed in England a fortnight or so before Christmas, and I had just one worry – I was unemployed. Jobs helping with Christmas post that I used to do as a student had long since been snapped up, so I found myself a post as a waitress in a Tettenhall hotel which was taking on extra staff for the festive rush of lunches and dinners.

Fortunately, most of the customers at that time of year didn't care too much what they ate, or how it was served, as long as they had plenty to drink. I settled into the job quite well and was feeling rather proud of myself in my new role until a couple of unfortunate incidents convinced me that I was not cut out to be a star waitress.

Once, while serving mashed potatoes, I brought the spoon back to the dish with a large lump of potato still clinging to it. It dropped off with a great plop – not on to the floor, but right down the bare back of a rather portly lady who leapt to her feet with a shriek.

Another night, I collected a tray of fifteen liqueurs from the bar downstairs and prepared to sprint back up the steps to the restaurant, thinking I would be keeping fit for hockey by doing so. Unfortunately, I got no farther than the first step. I tripped, the tray flew upwards to crash against the ninth step, and I lay at the bottom catching the drips!

After Christmas, I was able to develop my new-found liking for ten-pin bowling by taking a job in a new bowling centre which had opened in Wolverhampton during my stay in the States. Again, it was hardly taxing, helping at the counter, handing out shoes and offering a little advice to the rank beginners. It had its funnier side on the nights when I was required to work late. I could always tell when the pubs had shut by the rapid deterioration in standards. I particularly remember one man, decidedly the worse for drink, who released his ball awkwardly and saw it shoot off across the entrances to twenty other lanes instead of down his own lane, skittling the patrons instead of the pins.

At Easter, I was jobwise on the move again. I took a summer-term job at Bournville College of Further Education – on the outskirts of Birmingham. Swimming and tennis were the two main sports I taught here, and many of my pupils were on day-release from the Cadbury's factory over the road, which at least provided me with plenty of cheap chocolate.

I had suffered a major disappointment by this time. I was picked for Staffordshire on my return from America, but I just could not produce my best form and I failed to gain selection for the England team. I had managed to keep my place in the Midlands team over Hazell Feltwell and played in all four games; Hazell appeared in two Midlands 'B' matches and when sides were named for an England final trial game, my name was missing and Hazell had leap-frogged into that trial. Although I knew I was not playing my best I thought it strange that I had not been dropped within the Midlands and replaced by Hazell Feltwell if she was playing any better. The match that cooked my goose was when Midlands played the West; in one frantic West attack I nearly split in half making a save at full stretch and as I lay in a sprawl I attempted to push the ball round the post with my

stick out of the way of the hungry West forwards. I then
proceeded to play the best cricket sweep of my hockey
career and thumped the ball – not round the post, but into
my own goal! Fool! So with that cricket shot I swept out of
hockey into cricket!

Hazell however, for whom I have great respect and admiration, won her England place and was to keep it for the
next ten years. The reason I felt I was not playing well was
that having written my hockey goalkeeper's book, I found I
was trying too hard to carry out what I had written; I've
decided I'm perhaps better playing by light of nature and
instinct instead of being wrapped up in my deepest thoughts!

10 World Cup

Women are not always second-best in the game of cricket. It was women after all, who staged the first ever Cricket World Cup – an idea born out of a few after-dinner brandies on a night in 1971. But I can't honestly claim any credit for the idea. It was the exclusive brainchild of our dear friend, Jack Hayward.

The Haywards were in England at the time, and I happened to be staying with them in their Sussex home, during a weekend of women's cricket at Eastbourne. On the day in question, I had been captaining England against Young England before returning to have dinner with Jack and Jean. Then, with my appetite satisfied and brandy glass in hand, we sat and talked into the wee small hours as Jack tried to dream up some new method of helping the women's game.

The idea came quite naturally, really. 'Why', he asked, 'couldn't we bring every national women's team to England for a World Cup competition?' I was staggered by the idea which he had conjured up, but gingerly asked if he had any idea what such a venture might cost. After a few moment's thought, he said, 'Yes, around £30,000!' He was still set on the scheme, however. We sat and talked over all the possibilities of the innovation and reached the overriding conclusion that it would be marvellous to beat the men's cricket to the punch and stage the first-ever World Cup of cricket. This was not something that could be staged as a private enterprise, though. It had to be channelled through the correct authorities, and we felt that it would be fitting if Jack broached the idea with the WCA.

In true Hayward style, he wasted no time. In the next day's game on the Eastbourne ground, I was leading my own women's eleven against a BBC men's side, and while we were in the field, I noticed Jack arrive. He immediately sought out the association's chairman and led her off to a couple of seats near the sightscreen, where they sat, deep in conversation, for some time; I tried to concentrate on our game but would have loved to be a fly with good hearing on that sightscreen. The response from the WCA was overwhelmingly in favour. The first World Cup in cricket history was written in for 1973, leaving only eighteen months to organise it.

Jack Hayward finally paid £10,000 more than his original estimate, but didn't appear to begrudge a penny of it. Someone once asked him, a little scathingly, why he ploughed so much of his money into women's cricket. 'It's quite simple,' he replied. 'I love women, and I love cricket – and what could be better than to have the two rolled together!'

The months dividing thought and action on the World Cup front saw no significant deceleration in my own life-style. But it did see some changes.

In the spring of 1972, I left the *Wolverhampton Express and Star*, where even my part-time job had become more and more difficult to fit in. I was becoming steadily more involved in freelance writing for the *Daily Telegraph*, both on women's hockey and cricket, and this, together with radio and television work, speaking engagements and a promotional job with a sports shop chain, was more than enough to leave me in need of a few Bob Martin condition powders to stave off exhaustion.

I had written for the *Telegraph* during England's tours of Australia and the West Indies. In Australia, it was never a problem, as the time difference allowed me a clear twelve hours to compose a report. But in the Caribbean I was stretched to the limit. They are five hours behind British time, which means that at about the time play is finishing for the day, Fleet Street newspapers are sweating on the deadline for their last editions!

More work was coming my way from both radio and television, and October 1972 was an exciting month. Apart from being shocked by my appointment as the first woman sports reporter for ITV's 'World of Sport', I also made my debut on the BBC radio show 'Petticoat Line'. This was something which had appealed to me for some time, and I'd managed to enquire, through a BBC producer friend, whether there was any hope of my getting a chance. Eventually, I was called to London to see the 'Petticoat Line' producer, who seemed particularly interested in my anecdotes of the various cricket tours I had been on. After relating some of the 'stranger than fiction' ones to him, he agreed to try and give me a spot on the show. My chance arrived in October.

'Petticoat Line' was a long-running panel programme on which four women answered listener's letters on the air with the aim of working in some stories of their own and building an amusing, entertaining show. The panel I was to be part of included Teddy, one of the singing Beverley Sisters, Baroness Stocks, and Renée Houston, Chief Petticoat and a resident on the show. I was 'all-of-a-quiver' before going on the air, but Renée, whom I admired enormously as a remarkably strong and talented lady who was then seventy years of age, showed me genuine kindness. Putting her hand on my shoulder, she said: 'You'll get very nervous when you get out on the stage, my dear; be sure to go to the lavatory first!'

My other work was widely diversified. In television, I appeared on a Tyne-Tees chat show and more than ever I felt the ambition to have one of my own! I presented several sport spots for ITV and ATV in the Midlands, and after persistent nagging became the subject of a Frank Bough tea-time interview during a John Player League match at Leicester covered by BBC 2.

I had learned that work in the media rarely comes to those who don't ask – at least at first – but constantly badgering everyone in power did land me one or two different jobs, such as commentating on a netball match for ATV, and going back to Buckingham Palace to compere a garden party stage-show for disabled war veterans, arranged annually by Anona Winn.

Dinner speaking still occupied an amazing number of my evenings, with invitations coming in from all sorts of clubs and societies. At one luncheon in London, when I agreed to speak to the Association of Newspaper Circulation Managers another challenge cropped up. It was during a time of power workers' disputes, and just as I was being introduced and preparing to shuffle to my feet and my notes, the lights went out. I had to appear by candlelight – very romantic!

Cricket itself was taking me into a variety of environments, ranging from a place in the wives' team again for the annual Royal Ascot match against the racing writers, to selection for Ed Stewart's Showbiz XI playing at the elegant Blenheim Palace.

I also captained the only women's side in the Sussex County Cricket Club's Six-a-Side Competition at Hove, when we walked off with the prize for the most entertaining side, and played against the team of government officials and civil servants' called Mandarins. We also went to Newmarket for a Lord's Taverners match, during which Clement Freud was extremely upset at being dismissed in his second over for a lowly score and left in high dudgeon!

Perhaps the oddest cricket day of 1972 was in the small Sussex village where Jack Hayward has his home. I had taken a side down there to play the village club, and it just happened to be the day that Alan Whicker chose to interview me for his 'Whicker's World' programme on women in unusual occupations.

Under any other circumstances, the match would have been called off without a second thought, because the monsoon season seemed to have set in. Muddy puddles covered the square and outfield, but just because Alan Whicker needed a cricket background for the filming, the teams had to go through a farcical pretence of staging a game. What was even dafter was that although I sat out in the deluge for half-an-hour being interviewed, the eventual showing cut me down to about five minutes and I looked as though I had gone through a car wash without my car!

Finally, and not without preliminary problems, the World Cup arrived. Seven teams were to take part – England, Young England, Australia, New Zealand, Jamaica, Trinidad and Tobago, and an International XI.

The inclusion of the last collective side may be surprising, but it had been hoped that a few South Africans could play in the International XI. Unhappily, politics won again. The West Indian teams threatened to withdraw if any South Africans played, and we were advised that it would be an unwise and potentially disruptive move, so the WCA were forced to back down. We therefore gathered a multi-national side comprising players who had not quite got into their own country's senior squad.

The entire competition was run on a league basis, with each team playing everyone else in sixty-over matches. In retrospect, this may have been an error of organisation from which we were lucky to emerge unscathed. It only worked out because England and Australia met in the final match with the Cup still undecided; the concluding match could have been a complete anti-climax, had it not in effect been the crucial decider.

No tournament such as this, with so much cricket in such a confined schedule, can hope to succeed without the help of the weather. The first men's World Cup, two years later, was to be blessed with almost incessant sunshine. We were not so lucky.

New Zealand and England suffered most at the hands of rain. We, in fact, had three successive matches interfered with, and our fixture against New Zealand became a farce when, at a moment's notice, our target was cut from 106 in thirty-five overs to fifteen overs by which time we had only mustered 34 instead of the necessary 45 and so we lost the match – or rather the weather won the contest by a technical knock-out.

The opening match of the Cup, between Jamaica and New Zealand, had been washed out without a ball being bowled. I had driven up to the Kew ground from Royal Ascot, and as I studied the sodden scene I felt sorry for the West Indian girls who were bravely trying to keep warm on this 'flaming' June day!

Rain, however, influenced the fact that we achieved a perfect climax to the tournament, for Australia reached their penultimate match – against the Internationals at Swansea – needing a win to guarantee the Cup. They were foiled only by a downpour.

Edward Heath, as prime minister, gave all the teams a most splendid champagne reception at Number 10: I had made the request for such a gathering through his 'cricketing' private secretary Christopher Roberts. You can imagine the staggering effect on the snap-happy tourists who always throng Downing Street when they saw more than a hundred women cricketers invading the front door of the prime minister's residence. I'm sure many wondered if Britain's handsome bachelor PM was entertaining a harem!

So it all depended on the last match at Edgbaston, where the sun at last emerged after a misty start. It shone on England through the day, and after winning the toss we virtually put Australia out of the running with a sixty-over total of 279 for three, the highest score achieved throughout the competition.

Enid Bakewell, whose technique might have put a few men to shame, scored 118, with both Lynne Thomas and myself reaching half-centuries. I took four overs to get off the mark and although I was anxious, Derrick and several friends could not face the tension and they all bumped into one another at the back of the grandstand – escaping! It was all a bit much for the Aussies, and there was never much doubt that we would win.

They eventually fell 92 runs short, too many to make the closing overs at all exciting for the spectators. I bowled the last over and even I felt certain that Australia could not score 90-odd off my six deliveries. I paced out my run, turned to bowl and found that every one of my England team had placed themselves at least 70 yards out on the boundaries edge (including wicket-keeper Shirley Hodges) – such was their confidence in my bowling talent! Among the audience watching us from the gallery was Princess Anne, who, although never confessing to be a cricket fan, had kindly agreed to present the Cup. I felt almost guilty about the tame result. When she handed over the trophy, I apologised for 'delaying' her. She said she didn't mind in the slightest but I rather think she was being very gracious and diplomatic.

The following day England, as winners, took on a Rest of the World XI and beat them by seven wickets. This match was sponsored by John Haig, the whisky people, and afterwards some of the girls posed for photographs with bottles of Scotch given as awards cradled in their arms. It was a perfectly natural and harmless piece of public relations, but one or two of our mother-hen officials disagreed. They felt it was not the right image. I don't think that at the moment any minor concern like ours can afford to look a sponsor gift horse in the mouth, whether his products are cigarettes, babies' nappies or garden gnomes. Men's sport has seen the light and sponsors are crowding for space within their activities. Until we women adopt a similar attitude by welcoming sponsors – and, of course, promoting our own personalities to attract them – then I'm afraid we are always going to be struggling financially.

Jack Hayward paid for the first World Cup. It simply would not have happened without him. The second such event is being staged as I write this in 1978 – in India, the only country in which the women's game draws crowds and income of sufficient size to support it. Where will the next one be, I wonder – because people like Jack Hayward don't grow on trees.

11   Home Life

My parents considered me a lost cause in the marriage stakes and my former school and college friends thought me positively geriatric when I finally married at the age of thirty-two in 1971. It had not been a deliberate policy on my part to leave marriage so much later than the average girl, but perhaps it was just as well that I did! Neither had it been a case of my being left on the shelf – well, not quite!

Going back as far as my schooldays, I had always hoped that I would marry one day, but at that stage it simply was not the most pressing ambition in my life. I know some girls grow up with nothing more before their eyes than a suburban existence, with their husband's slippers placed lovingly in front of the fire before he turns up monotonously off the same commuter train every night. Socially, I was always happier when I had a boyfriend to go out with. It was comforting but, again, not a disaster if I lost him.

Marriage I discounted for years, chiefly on the grounds that it would have been unfair to my husband. I did not consider giving up cricket and hockey at an early age and settling down to mothering and housewifery. I knew it would take a man of extraordinary tolerance, understanding and – preferably – a sporting background of his own, to put up with my constant departures to various corners of the globe.

The question of marriage is different for a professional sportsman. Sport is his life and his living, and if he is lucky enough to be picked for an overseas tour, he is doing no more than furthering his career and, almost certainly, producing a better standard of living for his family. This is why in some ways it is difficult to blame cricketers who accepted the financial carrot dangled by Kerry Packer; a cricketer's lot is not a happy one in terms of remuneration. If only this Australian entrepreneur had not held a threatening pistol, in the form of large cash rewards for players, to the heads of world cricket.

For a woman such as I, though, cricket is an extravagant hobby.

When I did marry, it was not as a result of a lightning romance. I had known Derrick Flint for several years, both as a cricketer who had spent some time on the Warwickshire staff, and as an active member of the Wolverhampton squash club where I played. He was just one of our crowd. He had also been married before, so initially, while he was 'attached', I knew Derrick purely as a squash acquaintance with whom I might have shared a drink and his company as with all our group of friends.

I would never dream of threatening anybody's marriage by setting my cap at a married man, and I can say with complete honesty that I would never even consider having an affair with one. I always laugh at the pronouncement of a marriage guidance expert that two out of every six marriages end in divorce – and the other four just fight it out to the bitter end!

My upbringing has taught me a great respect for marriage and all that it means. In this modern age it seems just too easy to end a marriage, either in divorce or separation, but I am not one of those who celebrates the introduction of such an easy escape from marital responsibilities.

There have been, and always will be, married men who think of sportswomen like me as easy game, but they find me scornful of their approach. I would never wish to be thought of as an angelic puritan, (not that there is much danger of it!), but I do have principles which I stand by – and one of the strongest is that I refuse to take part in anything which could contribute to the break-up of a marriage.

Even after Derrick had been left on his own we did nothing more intriguing than play squash. We progressed from a platonic friendship only when the divorce action he had brought was completed. It was only then that I imagined that he could be the man I wanted to marry – and then hoped that the feelings were mutual!

It could have been considered an obstacle to us that Derrick had been left three children by his previous wife. But in fact, it was no obstacle at all. At the time, the girls Rowan and Hazel were seven and twelve respectively and Simon was thirteen. They were all sensible children, who understood the situation, and they have never shown any resentment towards me as a 'substitute'. I hate the word 'stepmother', I wish there was a nicer name, such as 'sub-mum'.

Once Derrick and I had decided that we wanted to marry, however, the children did have to be considered, and the only way in which we could find out if the family unit could be happily retained with my addition was for the five of us to take a holiday together. It worked without a hitch, helped, no doubt, by the fact that all three of the children love sport. Rowan is a fine swimmer and an above-average tennis player, Hazel plays good tennis and hockey, while Simon is a typical former public-school rugby player – tall and thick-set, and fond of beer!

We returned from our Mediterranean break during August and decided to marry. At my 'tender' age there was little point in dallying, and we became engaged in mid-September, when Derrick presented me with a super diamond and sapphire ring in a bold, modern setting – nothing delicate for my square, practical hands. I was oddly shy about the ring and the engagement, and when we went to a charity 'hop' at a nearby village hall that night, I wore the ring but neither of us mentioned the event to any of our friends. As we were helping ourselves to the buffet, midway through the evening, one of the men in our group noticed the ring and exclaimed: 'Hey, what's this with the rocks?' The secret was out, the word spread round the dance like a bush-fire and the night became a stream of champagne.

The party went on until four in the morning, but I was up

again at 7.30 and on the road for Silvertown, in East London, where I was leading my women's team in a cricket match against the ITV 'World of Sport' television side. I shall never forget the expressions on the faces of people like John Bromley, Dickie Davies, Brian Moore and Neil Durden-Smith when I turned up with my engagement ring displayed. I became very left-handed that day and I was a very happy soul, although decidedly hungover!

We were married on an unusually warm and sunny 1 November. I had wanted a simple white wedding; but we were unable to have a Church of England ceremony and I happily settled for the registry office, followed by a service of blessing in my local Penn Fields church. We emerged from the church through a tunnel of bats held up by several of the England team, almost all of whom had managed to take a day off work and travel up for the wedding. Then, after the traditional reception, family get-togethers and celebrations, we left for a honeymoon in Marrakesh and hit trouble – just for a change!

Our first night as Mr and Mrs Flint was spent in a hotel near Heathrow Airport, from where we were due to fly the next morning. When we woke and flicked on the radio, we were greeted by the news that no flights would be leaving Heathrow that morning due to an engineers' strike. Good start!

Passengers were advised to turn up at the airport, however, and after a few hours of idling, we were herded on to a coach with forty other people and driven to Gatwick. There, a Comet was produced from a hangar, they pumped up the tyres and dusted the wings and we set off for Marrakesh *only* six hours late.

Gibraltar was the first scheduled stop, but wild and windy conditions forced us to fly on to Tangier. Having landed there, we were stuck for the night, as Tangier airport had no facilities for night take-offs. So, with our 'adventure' improving by the minute, we were booked into a hotel in the dark, mysterious city.

There was more delay to come the next morning, when

our courier informed us that there were no flights to Marrakesh until Thursday, another twenty-four hours hence. As we had only booked for eight days anyway, this further snag produced some understandably irritable reactions. 'How', we demanded, 'can we get to Marrakesh'. The answer came back – catch a train!

So at midday, sixteen intrepid travellers including us two newly-weds from Wolverhampton, UK, were sitting on a railway platform in North Africa when a smart, American-style train drew in. Down through Casablanca we chugged, before changing trains at Rabat, and we were hurried across the platform by the stern voices of the guards. Quite what the hustling was for, I can't imagine, for our second train drew a yard or so out of the station and stopped for an hour!

Derrick and I were incarcerated in a sparse, bolt-upright leather-seated compartment with another young English couple called Pat and John. After bemoaning our fates, we settled down to drink the solitary refreshment that we could muster between us – one bottle of Scotch. There was no buffet on the train and the water was undrinkable, so we passed the bottle between the four of us and drank neat nips. By the time the train got under way, we had all downed a fair amount, and I was the first to fall asleep. John, sitting opposite me, dropped off next, but Derrick's efforts to sleep were somewhat interrupted. Pat, we found out later, was the sort of girl who just about managed a sherry at a wedding; Scotch was completely alien to her system, and while her husband and I slept through the night, Derrick was obliged to look after her as she was being regularly sick out of the train window. How romantic!

We arrived at Marrakesh at midday on Thursday, forty-four hours later than the intended arrival time, and to add to our frustration we soon discovered that we were visiting during the rainy season. It didn't say that in the brochure!

Back in England, I became a housewife and a 'sub-mum'. There were, as I've said, few problems in this transitional period of our lives. Becoming a stepmother can be a difficult operation as one always has the feeling that you can never be anything more than a substitute. It can be equally hard for the children, and I think it is especially difficult, physically and emotionally, for a girl fully to accept and appreciate a 'second mother'.

Discipline is the most delicate area. I realised immediately that I had to be careful here, as a strict, heavy-handed approach could have drawn wrathful cries of: 'Who are you to tell me that? You're not my mother!' Fortunately, all three children were receptive, and I think that even in the early days, they were aware of my difficulty. They certainly didn't play me up or give me much call to hand out punishments.

Derrick returned to his civil engineering and construction business; he had set this up himself with a partner, with a single digger and one lorry in the early 1960s, and nursed it along to its current state as a small but successful concern.

Unlike me, Derrick is a placid person who rarely loses his temper. Perhaps we are compatible because of our temperamental differences – I can fly off the handle at the slightest provocation – and I'm a great grumbler! He is certainly as keen on sport as I am, and has the background to justify it. His father, Ben Flint, and his uncle, Billy, both played cricket for Nottinghamshire, and Billy was also a professional footballer with Notts County. Derrick recalls that Trevor Bailey, Peter May and Doug Insole, all England players, were among his victims when he was a leg-break bowler for Warwickshire – such name-dropping!

Since then, Derrick has played club cricket in the Midlands for Harborne, Coventry and North Warwick and Wolverhampton, but he has now gone back to Edgbaston as captain and guiding light of the Warwickshire Colts side.

If the first two years of married life had been reasonably normal and quiet, everything changed for Derrick and me on the day in November 1973 when I discovered I was pregnant. I'm sure many people never imagine me having a baby; perhaps it was because they felt that I could never disrupt my sporting life, or perhaps it was because they felt I would never make a mum. Whatever the reasons, I was slightly self-conscious about the pregnancy: early reactions to the news included comments like 'Really! I never thought you would bother with that sort of thing' – motherhood, they meant!

Fortunately, I remained healthy, never suffering a day of morning sickness (except once, but that was due to port and not my portliness!). I was able to carry on writing and speaking almost up to the birth the following June. Hockey, however, was not quite the thing to play. I couldn't imagine the little embryo enjoying being bounced around as I kept goal every Saturday, so I gave the game up for a season and in some ways I found the break quite enjoyable. But watching two exciting sporting events almost gave me a miscarriage! One was in the Barbarians match against the New Zealand All Blacks in Cardiff, when the try of the decade was scored by Gareth Edwards – I was glued to the television screen; the other was watching Wolves play Leeds in the Third Round of the FA Cup at Molineux – Wolves all but won and the tension was so great I felt I might explode!

It was in 1974 that I began earnestly seeking sponsors for the 1976 visit of the Australians, and I went to the London offices of the Prudential Assurance Company during the first week of June, heavily pregnant. One of the directors, showing a polite interest, enquired when the happy event was due, and I had to stifle a laugh as he and his colleagues blanched visibly when I replied: 'Six days' time.' I'm sure they had visions of our meeting ending in chaos as I went into premature labour and they had to rush to put the water on to boil!

They needn't have worried. At three in the morning on 7 June, I was woken by twinges in my hinges. Derrick, trying to be extremely calm rushed me to New Cross Hospital in Wolverhampton, where it all turned out to be a false alarm!

Having got me in, however, the specialist, Clifford Newbold, decided that it was as good a time as any to induce the birth.

Above: 23 'If I ruled the world . . .' Holding aloft the World Cup won by England at Edgbaston and made a royal occasion by the presence of Princess Anne. The gallery is lined with my family and friends and Jack Hayward and his family. Below: 24 '. . . Let no man put asunder.' Rival (?) captains Denis Compton and RHF at the Oval in 1973 for Old England Men v. 'Younger' England Women – the first time ever that opposing captains kissed one another before the game started

Above: 25 Receiving the Guild of Professional Toastmasters' Best After-dinner Speaker Award in 1973 from the previous winner, the late and great Graham Hill – one of my sporting heroes. *Below:* 26 At Hove CC with the late Jim Gillman, grand old man of cricket and last surviving cricketer who played with W G Grace

Above left: 27 Captains all at Number 10: three women's cricket captains, Louise Brown (Trinidad and Tobago), Yolande Geddes (Jamaica) and myself with Edward Heath (*Morning Cloud*). *Top right:* 28 Pre-Ascot post-cricket match fruit cake and champers with Lord Oaksey (Marlborough of the *Daily Telegraph*). *Below:* 29 'I must feed the dog' – Cracker, our devoted Labrador, who bats at number three

Above: 30 Jokers are wild. Henry 'Splash it all over' Cooper throws a hilarious punch-line to cricketers (left to right) Freddie Titmus, Colin Cowdrey and RHF before a sports stars' motor race at Brands Hatch. *Below:* 31 Stretching the imagination, among other things! RHF in goal for Staffordshire, 1975

They began the attempt at midday on the 7th. At midnight, after twelve hours of fruitless labour, they gave it up. My 'sporty' muscles would not relax enough, so a caesarian birth was ordered.

As I was wheeled into the theatre, dopy from the growing effect of an injection, a chatty nurse asked me if I had decided on a name for the baby if it was a boy. Without looking up, I mustered what I thought was a good answer. 'Enoch,' I joked, referring to the former MP from Wolverhampton, Enoch Powell, who spoke so harshly his views on the immigrant population of Britain. The roars of laughter from everyone around me seemed an exaggerated response to my corny reply, so I opened my eyes and discovered the reason. The nurse was black and beautiful; one of Mr Powell's West Indian 'friends'. Fortunately, she had seen the funny side and was laughing more than anyone!

I remember nothing more until I partially came round, saw the shape of a nurse and heard her tell me that I had produced a healthy boy. Relieved and happy, I closed my eyes and drifted back to sleep.

Throughout the pregnancy, I had insisted, to myself and to others, that I had no preference for a boy or girl. Subconsciously, however, I think I always wanted a boy as there was far more chance of him becoming the sort of rough, tough sportsman that I knew I would enjoy.

We chose the first name Benjamin because we both liked it and it happened to be Derrick's father's name. Giles became the second name because my son reminded me of one of the cartoonist's famous shrivelled characters during his first weeks in the world. And Heyhoe is his third name. My father's family were keen to perpetuate the name, and anyway, we convinced ourselves that all the best amateur cricketers in the good old days had three initials before their name!

I stayed in hospital for a fortnight after the birth, and I must say it couldn't have been planned better. Derrick brought in a portable television set, and in those two weeks I managed

E

to watch the World Cup, an England *v.* Pakistan Test Match, Wimbledon and Royal Ascot. Benjamin, lying in his crib facing the set, was thus given an early and concentrated introduction to the sporting life!

Dramatic changes were now inevitable in my life, although I had honestly never really realised just how time-consuming babies could be. After bringing up three children from his first marriage, Derrick was extremely nifty with the nappies, but the problems arose when both he and I were out on business. It was fortunate that we were able to call on our home help during the mornings, and employ a friend of ours to baby-sit through the afternoon hours if we were both away for the day. Even now though, if humanly possible, I aim to get back to 'home base' at night after any professional engagement so that I can give as much 'mothering-time' as possible to Benjamin.

I had set myself a target of a return to active cricket within three months of becoming a mother. In fact, I managed it within two – spurred on by the incentive of leading the England women against an Old England men's side at the Oval in a special challenge match promoted by the *Evening Standard* newspaper. Rain eventually forced a cancellation, but only after I had made my grand entrance at the Oval, cricket-bag in one hand, carry-cot in the other. I parked Benjamin in the dressing-room while I had lunch with the players, leaving instructions with the dear old attendant, Ted, to keep an eye on him.

Half-way through the meal, Ted burst into the lunch room in a state of rare panic and announced that, for the life of him, he couldn't make the boy stop crying. I think poor old Ted had been more alarmed by my two-month-old son than by any of the Surrey players' demands during the season!

I made the decision to cut down on long-distance evening speaking engagements, initially to look after Benjamin, but also because I had grown rather weary of racing to and fro all over the country and throwing the odd jam butty at Derrick as I rushed in from one engagement before zooming off to another. Now the family came first.

In the summer, when both Derrick and I were playing cricket at weekends, Ben would come with me. It became a regular routine on a Saturday morning to pack the car with play pen, pot, clothes, toys, pram and food . . . just for a day's cricket! Bottle-feeding was obviously a necessity, because I could hardly nip off the field at the drinks interval to feed my son! I normally managed to get one of our player's mothers to look after young Flint and feed him while I was on the field, but in one game at Hastings this system caused some rare confusion.

As I was leading the side out to field, Lynne Thomas's mother, the baby-minder of the day, called from the pavilion: 'What time is lunch?' I turned and called back that it was 12.30, and as the game got under way, I noticed some heated arguing going on between the scorers and some other officials. Apparently, one of the scorers had overheard me and assumed that I was referring to players' lunches rather than my own offspring. Our lunch was in fact set for 1.30 p.m. and the scorer was struggling to fathom out how I had got my wires crossed!

During one match against a men's side in Notts, I looked up during my innings and spotted Derrick pushing Ben's pram around the boundary. It was an odd sight to me and I felt slightly perturbed. It wasn't right, I reasoned, that things were this way around. I wondered if Derrick was thinking the same, and that there ought to be a Men's Lib. for him.

Later on, when Ben had learned to toddle about, it often became difficult for me to get out to bat. He would cling on to me as I made a hopping attempt to get to the middle. It was even worse when he came to hockey and ran into the goalmouth behind me, just to say hallo!

My son is a very lively lad who never seems to need any sleep. We had to put a barricade on his door after finding him downstairs one morning at three o'clock, feeding biscuits to the dog. He had also poured himself a cupful of neat lime juice – that would have taken the smile off his face! Now, however, he can conquer the barricade – because it's there, I suppose. In order to scramble over, he piles up his stuffed animals which act as a sort of springboard for his mountaineering.

I have mentioned Ben's early indoctrination into sport – even at his tender age he can recognise Virginia Wade when she comes on to the TV screen, and last summer, when it was time for the Test interval at 4.20 p.m. and Mike Brearley led off his merry men, Benjamin commented that they were going into the '*palivion* for tea'! His selection of toys obviously in cludes cricket bat, rugby ball, hockey stick and football – which leads me to think he might hate sport later!

Ben was three-and-a-half years old when I took a team to Canada in 1977 to join in the Toronto Men's Cricket Club 150th anniversary celebrations. We had turned the tour into a family holiday, and Derrick, Rowan and Benjamin were sitting on the boundary as I went out to bat in one of the games. After giving Benjamin a farewell kiss, I light-heartedly called, 'Won't be long,' specifically to him but perfectly audible to all the spectators around.

I was right. A few balls later, I was out for one, and my son and heir was delighted. Rushing out to meet my stern-faced trudge, he shouted: 'You didn't get many runs, did you mummy?' The crowd laughed, and even I managed to produce a smile in my misery!

12 MBE

John, Paul, George and Ringo sent their MBEs back to the Palace. Many other recipients, I suppose, have put them away in a never-to-be-opened drawer. But when I received my medal from the Queen in 1972, it was one of the greatest moments of my life. I know it sounds hackneyed to rattle on about what an unexpected and thrilling surprise it all was, but it's true! When notification of the award was given to me in April, I found it impossible to believe.

On the morning when the letter arrived, I was alone in the house. It was just five months after our wedding, Derrick was at his office on the other side of Wolverhampton and I was making a pretence at being a housewife when Dora, our faithful postlady, dropped the mail through the letter-box. One letter looked curiously interesting. 'On Her Majesty's Service' in the top left-hand corner normally indicates a bill or tax demand of some sort. This one was different for two reasons. First, the envelope was white instead of the brown ones which contain tax demands and second, it had four significant words in the bottom left-hand corner – 'Urgent', 'Personal', and 'Prime Minister'. My eyebrows raised several inches.

Having decided it was probably not a bill, my 'think-tank' told me that it was almost certainly from one of the prime minister's secretaries, whom I had met at the reception for Ray Illingworth's Ashes-winning England team at 10 Downing Street twelve months earlier. He was probably making a request for a match which I had promised. This particular secretary organised a wandering cricket team called the Mandarins, made up of civil servants and diplomats. That, I thought, had to be the explanation.

It wasn't from him at all, as I discovered as soon as my eyes met the heading just below the Downing Street address. 'HONOURS', it announced boldly. 'IN CONFIDENCE'. At first reading, I scarcely took in the contents of the letter at all. I had to go through it again, straining to take in the information that the prime minister intended to include my name in his nominations to the Queen for the MBE in her birthday honours list.

To be rational at a time like this is impossible. Anyway, that's my only excuse for bellowing a resounding 'Whoopee!' to the rafters and cavorting around the kitchen in a dance of triumph. The house was not quite empty and so, desperate to boast to somebody, I hunted out its other occupant. She wasn't impressed at all by the news. In fact, she gave me a doleful, disapproving stare which suggested she considered I was just plain cuckoo. Cracker, our faithful old Labrador, sniffed the air with disdain!

Having already broken the confidence to Cracker's ears and got no response, I have to admit I rushed to the phone and called Derrick. I was so overcome by it all that he completely failed to understand my babblings at first. When I was able to slow down and enunciate, he finally got the message – and thought I was pulling his leg.

It also occurred to me that this could be some kind of practical joke by some high-spirited friends, but a closer study of the Downing Street paper convinced me it was authentic, and I eventually managed to convince myself that it was true.

For my next, and last, breach of the prime minister's confidence, I telephoned my mother. I may have been in a slightly calmer state by then, and I think I was audible when I told her the news. Complete silence greeted my announcement and I thought for a moment that the line had been cut off. But it was just that my mother was speechless with pride; next day she showed this in a touching way by sending me an Interflora spray of flowers.

I was so genuinely thrilled and honoured that what I had done for the game of women's cricket had been recognised in this way. It seemed to make all the hard work, all the disappointments worthwhile – although I never even dreamt that such an award should come my way for doing something which I almost looked on as a hobby!

I am a great believer in the monarchy. I have tremendous admiration for all the Royal Family and marvel at what they do and the manner in which they do it. Frankly, those who mock, criticise and despise 'the Royals' make me furious, and I would go as far as to say that Willie Hamilton's ridiculous speeches against the Family, in the Commons and elsewhere, must run very close to the borders of treason.

Having satisfied my excitement by telling Derrick and my mother, I then kept the secret. The official announcement of the honours list was to appear on the morning of Saturday, 3 June, and when Derrick and I went to the squash club for our regular Friday night drink on 2 June, we were, so far as I knew, the only people present in possession of the secret. I was wrong – again!

Tony Griffiths, one of our most active club committee men, had a lot of contacts in the press, who, of course, are always given an advance list of those people who are to be honoured. The news had been leaked to Tony, and at eight o'clock, shortly after our arrival at the club, he produced the night's first bottle of champagne. There seemed no point in trying to keep the secret any longer, so we all embarked on a super night of celebrating, switching the venue to our house when the club bar closed.

At one minute past midnight, Derrick conducted a mock investiture, and hung a wooden MBE around my neck. He had gone to the trouble of having it carved and inscribed by his carpenter, and although the whole thing was a bit of a joke, I have kept that wooden medal – with *almost* as much reverence as the real thing.

The authentic investiture was not until November, but the

thought of it was a constant spur in the five intervening months. Women are allowed to take two guests (men, for some reason, are permitted three) and, naturally enough, Derrick and my mother came to London with me. We booked into a hotel just around the corner from Buckingham Palace on the eve of the ceremony, to save fraying my nerves any further with travel problems the next morning. In the evening we went to a show and I forgot my anxiety as we watched an hilarious Lesley Phillips comedy *The Man most Likely to* . . .

November 8 dawned dry, crisp and clear – just right for my special day. We grandly took a taxi for the short ride from the hotel to Buckingham Palace, and I was a dithering mass of nerves.

Cars were allowed through the first set of gates, and I felt puffed up with pride as we passed the guards and motored into royal territory. There were almost two hundred people to be invested and the occasion was grand and vast; I'm only sorry now that nervousness prevented me from taking it all in, for I was many times more shaky than ever before any Test match innings.

Inside the building came the parting of the ways; Derrick and my mother branched off to the ballroom while I was shown into a large gilt room where all the people waiting for medals were separated into categories . . . knights, CBEs, OBEs, MBEs, etc.

It was, of course, etiquette for the honoured women to wear a hat and gloves; I felt rather self-conscious, so rarely is it that I crush a hat on to my head. I had on a beige wool tunic outfit and a silk blouse, topped by a hat that Derrick insisted I had borrowed from John Wayne – anything to boost my confidence!

In our groups, we were gradually ushered through the corridors until we filed, six at a time, across the top of the investiture hall. All the time we were lulled by an orchestra in the gallery. I glanced one way and saw the Queen carrying out her duties; I glanced the other and caught sight of Derrick and mother and I just about managed a smile, although my face felt stiff with nerves.

Then we were taken down a side corridor, made a sharp right-turn and there ahead I could really see the Queen. We stood in line waiting for our turn. At last it was me, and I took six paces forward before turning to my left, as instructed, to face the Queen. An usher called out, 'Heyhoe . . . Rachael Flint'.

My eyes began watering with unashamed emotion; I was so close to Her Majesty that I felt a ridiculous urge to call out, 'Hallo, Queen. How are you?' Getting a grip on myself, however, I advanced another six paces, knees knocking, body quivering, and delivered a wobbly curtsey at the Queen's knees. I thought, any minute now my hat will wobble straight down over my eyes!

Her adviser, at her elbow, whispered briefly in the Queen's ear, just to let her know who I was I suppose, before we shook hands. We had been given the option of keeping our gloves on or taking them both off. I had chosen the bare hand as the Queen was wearing no gloves and I wanted to feel that I had really shaken hands with her.

I had not known whether to expect a conversation with the Queen or not, all I knew was that etiquette demanded that you wait until you are spoken to. True to form, the Queen had a few words with everyone. Leaning forward confidentially, she began: 'I understand you play cricket?' In my dithering state, it was as much as I could muster to reply with an Oscar-winning 'Yes, ma'am.' After asking how long I had been playing for England and getting some sort of stumbling response, she said: 'You obviously enjoy it, but don't you get very tired?' I managed my only worthy answer with: 'I'm not often at the crease long enough for that!' The Queen smiled, the charming royal smile that has melted millions, then she nodded gently to signify that my unforgettable moment was at an end. Another curtsey, a few awkward steps backwards, and I joined the rest of the recipients with their medals.

It is not easy to put into words just what the honour means to me, but I think now, after the shock of losing the England captaincy, I probably cherish it more than ever. I find it ironic to think back and reflect that it was awarded 'for services to women's cricket'. Someone within the game must have approved my nomination – perhaps one of the very people who, five years later, were to be instrumental in shattering an important and dear part of my life.

The medal itself is mounted on pink and grey ribbon, with the crown on one side of the medal and the lettering on the other. Some friends of ours insist that MBE stands for Mitchell and Butler's Export, (a Midland brew of ale) and that it must have been awarded for 'services to beer drinking'!

It isn't the sort of thing you put round your neck for a trip to the pub, and I admit I wear it very rarely. But on one occasion when it was requested was at a very high-class military ball, I played a little practical joke and wore round my neck a mock 'CDM' of silver and purple ribbon and a six-penny bar of Cadbury's milk chocolate of the kind that Cadbury's were putting out in an advertising campaign of the time. A very crusty old colonel was fascinated by my medal, and when he peered short-sightedly at the resplendent display and asked rather pompously what it had been awarded for, I kept a straight face and told him that it was for 'services to the eating of chocolate'!

One other occasion when I wear my MBE is on Christmas Day. We have a tradition at home that presents wait until after lunch and the Queen's three o'clock speech is over. So when the debris is cleared away, and the whole family sit down eyeing the presents, I pin on my medal and sit with a daft grin on my face, watching 'my' Queen give her Christmas message to the world and me.

13 Television

Shortly before our first wedding anniversary, a phone call from 'World of Sport' producer Stuart McConachie asked me to go to London. Although I didn't know it at the time, that call was to bring my television ambitions to some sort of fruition. Television had always fascinated me, and ever since my first steps into the world of journalism, my aim had been to try to break into radio and television sports work.

My first television venture in sport was 'engineered' by Neil Durden-Smith and myself, early in 1970. Neil, who plays both cricket and hockey at a high level, was then the regular television commentator when ITV covered the annual women's hockey international at Wembley. When I met Neil at a Lord's Taverners match, conversation turned to television, and with a little prompting he agreed to do what he could to get me on as his summariser at Wembley. His tactics were unorthodox. He would not, he said, take the idea to the station's powers. Instead, he proposed to 'smuggle' me in on the day itself and hope that everyone approved of his initiative.

It all began to go wrong on the Wednesday night prior to the game, when a deluge of rain made the international doubtful. Further rain the next day confirmed the worst, and late on Thursday morning, the England-Australia international was officially called off.

I thought it a desperately premature decision by the Wembley authorities yet indicative of the place that women's hockey holds in their priorities. A week earlier, the Football League Cup Final had been staged at Wembley, and the pitch had been covered with straw for a day to save it from frost, before hundreds of volunteers came in on Saturday morning to clear it for action. All that effort for football, but for hockey – not a finger lifted.

It was not the political side of the decision which so depressed me, though, but the fact that my television debut looked likely to be called off with it. Defeat never comes easily to me, however, and after a chat with the then Women's Hockey Association's press officer, Joyce Clark, who in turn spoke to her president, we set out to find an alternative venue for the fixture.

I tried Lord's and the Oval, who both said it was too short notice to put on such an event. Chelsea, the only major London soccer ground unoccupied on the Saturday, gave a similar reply. It was Neil Durden-Smith who came up with the answer – White City, the vast bowl now underneath the M40 flyover which has probably been tagged a white elephant more times than any other sports stadium in the world – quite unjustifiably.

Lengthy but rapid negotiations finally brought success. On Friday afternoon White City agreed to stage the match. The problems, though, were only just beginning. It was all very well switching the venue, but if 60,000 spectators were not told, the whole affair would be a bit pointless. We contacted national press and radio stations to get the switch put out on their sports bulletins, but even with their co-operation, Saturday lunchtime saw absolute chaos in West London.

Coach-drivers carrying dozens of St Trinian-style girls in their vehicles headed blithely for Wembley. I can imagine their feelings on arrival there, relieved that their ordeal was over, only to be diverted another ten miles south-west!

The traffic around White City was at an almost complete standstill, and I was one of the thousands caught up in it. I arrived in the ground, breathless, and plonked myself down next to Neil on the commentary platform to the silent but obvious surprise of the floor manager.

As White City's capacity is much smaller than that of Wembley, there were inevitable seating problems. But the

match did take place, and I did make my first mark on a
television audience, albeit a small one. Neil and I had worked
hard for the chance, but it was worth it!

Since our successful tour of Australia, I had been sought
after to make various appearances and invited to countless
dinners. In the interests of my promotion fetish I attended as
many as my job and energy allowed. After the unofficial but
newsworthy tour of Jamaica in 1970 however, I was in even
greater demand, and the *Sunday Times* sent Norman Harris,
one of their sports staff, to interview me for a magazine
article. He spent an entire day with me, following me through
my journalism at the *Express and Star* and a session at the
Wolverhampton Cricket Club nets, where he bowled to me
himself. The day was completed with a chat over dinner at
The Rendezvous, one of Wolverhampton's stylish restaurants.

I had made a particular effort to put over the 'right' image.
I had tried to behave faultlessly all day and I was feeling
rather pleased with myself when the shish kebabs I had ordered
arrived at our table. Something had to go wrong and it did.
As I slid the food off the prong on to my plate of rice, the
prong slipped and a pile of meat and rice landed in my lap. I
cursed violently, a day's work was ruined, and so was my
dress! Norman Harris turned a blind eye!

My radio work increased with a spot on Pete Murray's
popular 'Open House' show and a sports forum in Reading in
which I made chairman Peter West puff rather hastily at his
perennial pipe with another *faux pas*. One of the questions to
the panel concerned the possibility of rigging fights in professional boxing and was obviously directed at the recent
farcical Muhammad Ali win when Sonny Liston had been
knocked out in the first round and many thought he had
taken a dive. In trying to make my feelings plain without
outwardly saying the fight was a nonsense, I chose my words
carefully! 'Good heavens,' I said, 'I wouldn't mind lying down
for that amount of money'!

Shortly after my hockey experience at White City, I

appeared on the BBC quiz show 'A Question of Sport'. The night before the recording, I had had a reunion dinner with Mick Lester, a cricketer whom I had met in New Zealand. I can only assume that the prawn cocktail was off, because I contracted a nasty dose of food poisoning and it made my face terribly swollen by the time I arrived at Manchester to go before the cameras – in fact it looked as if I had fought Muhammad Ali!

This time I got through without being the target of laughter, but a boxer in the opposition team didn't. During the section in which sports stars have to be identified, the screen flashed up a picture of Virginia Wade. The boxer had no doubts, though – he identified the tennis player as Pancho Gonzales!

At the tail-end of 1970, I met ITV's 'World of Sport' chiefs McConachie and John Bromley at the *Daily Express* Sportsman of the Year lunch. John later travelled back on the train to Birmingham with me and sounded me out about doing some television work. But, although I was again Neil Durden-Smith's summariser at Wembley the following March – this time officially – I was not seriously called on until that phone call from McConachie in October 1972.

He said he wanted to see me at the programme's London office to 'discuss ideas'. Not really knowing what to expect, I arrived to be met by both Stuart and John and ushered into an office 'to meet one or two people'. To my amazement, I found that this was a press launching of the 'World of Sport' decision to appoint me as their first female sports reporter. Thrown in at the deep end, I now had to defend myself against a barrage of questions from the press. I struggled until someone asked me if there were any sports I didn't enjoy. 'Yes', I replied. 'Women wrestling in mud.' Why not? 'Because I don't like the mud.'

I was put up in a most palatial suite at the Savoy Hotel for the night and thrust into my first professional television 'slot' the next day. The idea was that I should make about one contribution each month, featuring the obvious angles of women in sport and the more diverse ones. I did a piece on korfball – a mixed sport, a cross between soccer and netball – and one on women's soccer for which I had to go to pitch 79 on Wandsworth Common, in the lee of the prison.

I enjoyed the work because it was what I had wanted to do. But somehow I struggled to feel completely at ease. It was a vicious circle really, for I believe I would have done better with more regular work, but time, space and money would not allow this.

My annual Christmas 'treat' was to present the book review slot. After doing it once, I asked if in future I could have the books a few weeks in advance and prepare my own script. This never happened; someone else prepared the reviews and all I did was read off an autoscript, someone else's words on some books I had never even seen. It was difficult to be convincing and natural.

I think my best moments came when I was given freedom to interview someone. Graham Hill was my favourite subject. Virginia Wade was more difficult to interview, but once we had both relaxed it was a most enjoyable meeting.

Muhammad Ali in all his might and majesty came to the 'World of Sport' studios, and I was one of two women posted in the audience and primed with a question to ask the great man.

I realise that many more people dislike Ali than love him, but I happen to be one of his fans, and this was a big moment for me. I had noticed early in the cross-talk that his eyes could sparkle and laugh when he was asked questions which he wanted to answer, but they could burn fiercely at any he resented. Looking down at my prepared question, I felt more than a little hot around the gills!

My turn arrived. 'If you hadn't been so beautiful', I began, 'would you still have been the greatest?' For an awful moment, his eyes flashed anger at a question that was, in retrospect, rather cheeky. Then he softened just as suddenly, perhaps thinking that I was only a woman, anyway. His answer was perfectly civil: 'No, certainly not, ma'am,' and I was just too scared to ask him anything else.

My 'World of Sport' career lasted three years before my engagements and appearances began to decrease, possibly because my presentation had not been what they had hoped. I remember a producer once saying to me as I prepared to deliver a piece to the cameras: 'Come on, let's see the real Heyhoe on this.' And I think this was what was missing, mainly because of my lack of television experience and only having limited opportunities to improve my presentation. I haven't given up by any means, however, and I still dream that I might one day be given a chance on my own chat show – the female Michael Parkinson, with a less devoted attitude to Yorkshire cricket!

It is still an annual 'fixture' for me to assist the commentator at the Wembley hockey international, and I have to confess that there are times when a lack of knowledge of the game is shown by some of the men. One or two who have been used were watching the sport for the first time – and it showed! I have never done a main commentary and I'm not sure a woman ever should. Vocally, we have neither the tone nor the intonation to create the sporting feeling and drama that men can. For all that, though, viewers have missed a lot at these Wembley games: a couple of the men I have worked with on the game have been excellent commentators in their own right, but lacking any background in hockey or even any full knowledge of the game – Neil Durden-Smith excepted. I once had to prop up two clip-boards between myself and a new commentator and point to the name of the girl in possession – he knew none of them by sight. And to help another commentator who was hazy on the rules I had to write out the eight most obvious fouls on a piece of card and point to the relevant offence whenever there was a stoppage.

My funniest moment on the Wembley commentary point, however, came with Neil Durden-Smith, whom I could never fault on his knowledge of the game or its players. This was my first official spot as his assistant – Wembley, 1971 – and in the early stages I had done nothing but light cigarettes for him. During the course of the game, in a flurry of goalmouth action, Neil became so excited that the metal chair, which was fitted on a wooden plinth, shot from underneath him. His lip microphone went the other way and Neil himself crashed backwards! Retrieving the mike, I delivered a minute-of-recovery commentary, desperately trying not to laugh at the shaking bundle of sheepskin picking himself off the floor. I was tempted to stand on him and then I could have taken complete control and my solo debut would have been achieved!

Another hilarious occasion we shared was when Neil and I were commentating in the England v. Holland game. There was a trap – and Neil fell right into it: one Netherlands player was in possession and Neil, adding a little to the moment, said, 'So-and-so in possession is a medical assistant and has fifty-two Dutch caps'!

14   Journalism

There was no such thing as a sex discrimination law when I took my first steps into journalism and I soon became aware of a system which often frowns disapprovingly over the intrusion of women into the 'male domain' of sport.

Writing has always been a most enjoyable part of my life. I have been, and still am, in the almost unique position of simultaneously playing and writing about cricket and hockey. It has got me into some odd situations, and at times inflicted quite a strain on both sides of my sporting life. But it has given me a fascinating and valuable insight.

It all began in a minor sort of way in the mid 1960s. A Birmingham sports reporting agency run by a chap called Clive Everton, of world billiards fame, had occasionally employed me as a freelance writer on women's hockey, and it was this, coupled with my coaching tour of America, which provided the impetus for the writing of my coaching book on hockey goalkeeping. I had it privately printed, promoted it personally and enjoyed the whole operation enough to persuade me that journalism might have something for me.

Through a director friend of mine I rang the editor of the *Wolverhampton Express and Star* (in the top ten of provincial evening papers) and I insisted that they couldn't exist without a woman on their sports desk. I was not successful in my persuasion and I was left with the distinct impression that the sports editor at the time was not very enthusiastic about the idea of a female sports writer on his staff.

Having been refused, though, I asked in some desperation if they had any jobs at all on offer. I was, after all, out of work. After some thought, they told me that they were in the process of expanding their promotions department and could offer me a post as an assistant. It wasn't quite what I'd been hoping for, but it was better than either being penniless or returning to the teaching profession with which I had grown gradually disillusioned. So I accepted the offer, and in the true style of one who has been prone to many lucky breaks all my life, I had been working there no more than three weeks when the editor, Clement Jones, came through on the internal phone.

After such a short time in any job, the immediate reaction when the Big White Chief phones is one of panic. Although I couldn't recall any particular blunders, I assumed this was a call of reprimand if nothing worse. It came as a great surprise, therefore, when Clement Jones explained that the *Wolverhampton Chronicle*, the group's weekly paper, had just had a parting of the ways with their sports editor and could I possibly help fill two pages with sport for the next week or two? What a chance!

By the end of 1965, then, I had achieved another little ambition. I was, to all intents, a sports writer. What's more, the men working with me on the *Chronicle* were cricket-mad, which became a tremendous boon when I needed to plead for time off to play in various matches.

Within two years, I was transferred again, this time back to the *Express and Star* as a sports sub-editor, checking stories and helping with creating headlines, albeit mainly the column fillers. I felt a certain fulfilment – and also a certain amusement at the effect I was having on the rest of the sports desk.

As a lone woman around the desk, I was naturally delegated to tea-making and tidying duties, which I didn't complain about so long as the domestics didn't dominate my job. The amusing part, however, was that the men often found themselves checking their speech in mid-sentence, aware that I was present and not wanting to offend my ears with the sort of bad language that is part of most newspaper offices.

While on the *Chronicle*, I had regularly covered Wolves football, where I was something of a press outcast due to the

club's policy then of not allowing women in the press box. I
was instead given a free seat in the front row of the grandstand, which in fact afforded me a better view and greater
comfort than the rest of the writers sitting huddled in a box
that was, at the time, rather inadequate.

Before I get into any trouble with the club I still love, I
must hastily point out that not only have press facilities improved beyond recognition at the Molineux ground, but also
that I would now be allowed in the box !

When I transferred back to the *Chronicle* I gave up my
responsibility for Wolves until one day, when the regular
football writer was off, I was asked to go to Molineux and
cover the club's press call. This entailed going down with a
photographer, who would take shots of all the players, and
interviewing the manager and some of the players on prospects
for the coming season. A double-page spread in the centre of
the *Chronicle* was reserved, and I was detailed to write the
copy.

The part-time football writer was back in the office the
following day, and exploded with anger over the fact that I
had written this centre-spread and been given a by-line for it.
He seemed to believe that it was some evil plot of mine designed to upstage him, and he was purple with rage! Shouting,
'If you want to write the — football, you can!' he picked up
the wire filing tray and hurled it at me. Maybe he had forgotten my cricket training. Anyway, I was alert enough to
catch the tray in front of my eyes and throw it back at him,
which effectively calmed the argument.

This was the most explosive but certainly not the only
example of suspicion shown against me; I had great difficulty
in pinning down stories because many of the men I phoned
refused to believe I knew anything about sport. They were
probably accustomed to a man phoning them, to whom they
could pour out the story of their club's disasters and probably
spill a good story in the process. With me, they were altogether
more wary, and I had to develop the habit of throwing in the

odd knowledgeable phrase just to prove that I wasn't as dumb as they obviously believed.

In 1970, I rejected, somewhat reluctantly, the chance of joining the editorial staff of *The Cricketer* magazine. Much as I would have enjoyed magazine work, it simply would not have been possible to combine it with a full-time job elsewhere – and I was already stretching the tolerance of my superiors on the paper with all my time off.

That same year, however, I wound down my commitment with the *Express and Star* to a part-time basis and took up another appointment as promotions manager for a chain of sports shops in the Midlands. This work fitted in more easily with my married life which followed and was too much to allow me to continue as before with the paper. I also believed that the promotions job would provide me with another range of useful contacts for future years.

Throughout my time on the *Express and Star*, I was fighting a battle against the prejudices of the sports editor. He had nothing personal against me, but he refused to accept that women's sport in general was news, and therefore considered it unworthy of space in his paper. In many ways, I can understand his views. Both women in mainly-male sports and the distinctly female sports do not receive a great deal of publicity for one very valid reason – they lack the personalities which the public love, or, if they have them, they lack the know-how with which to promote them.

There have been recent exceptions. Gillian Gilks has put women's badminton in a prominent place, almost single-handedly producing greater coverage at all levels. What an irony that Gillian has run into a conflict with her game's authorities; I suppose her plight can be compared with my own in cricket. Perhaps her administrators were resentful of her growing bigger news-wise than the establishment.

Show-jumping and Three-Day Eventing have developed a massive following thanks to the exploits of the likes of Marion Mould, Janet Hodgson, Ann Moore and of course, Princess

Anne. I have the greatest admiration for Princess Anne who has reached the top in her sport, working against tremendous odds and difficulties. No wonder she occasionally crosses swords with the popular press who, instead of recognising her prowess as a horsewoman, are merely sitting there with cameras poised waiting for that sensational picture when she falls off. In male-dominated sports, personalities like Barry Sheene and Peter Collins have brought motor-cycling and speedway to the public through the media by their own insistent personalities.

It is all something of a vicious circle. The media will only take notice of minority women's sports if the sport has the personalities to promote. But until at least one part of the media takes a chance on a sport, who is to know whether the personalities exist or not? This is an argument I have since had several times with the *Daily Telegraph* in my constant if good-natured battle to win more space for women's hockey and cricket. I often complain that my report on the Wembley women's hockey international, watched by 60,000 people at the stadium and millions more on television, is granted less space than an account of a men's club match which might have been watched by a dozen people and a few dogs.

Just as the *Daily Express* indirectly promoted me in the speaking field, however, I have much to thank the *Telegraph* for in my journalistic career. Without receiving regular space and by-lines in their paper, I may well have missed out on other opportunities within the media, such as working for the BBC Radio Sports programmes, which included covering the first World Cup of women's hockey in Edinburgh in 1975.

While working for BBC Radio Sport, I attempted to employ the advantages of my feminine wiles – in the nicest possible way – to get an interview for 'Sport on Four', the Saturday morning sports programme hosted by Tony Lewis.

With Don Revie in disgrace and England searching for a new football manager late in 1977, everyone was tipping Brian

Clough – but nobody could get the once voluble man to talk about it. Having played cricket with him for the Lord's Taverners, I boldly phoned him at Nottingham Forest, and tried to exert my so-called charm. It didn't work but he couldn't have been nicer. 'Not even for you, my luv. They didn't want to listen to me five years ago, so they won't want to hear what I've got to say now.'

My relations with the press, both as a colleague and as a player, have been very happy – and I was so warmed by all the wonderful support they gave me when I lost my England captaincy. I couldn't have asked for a more loyal backing.

On the debit side though, when England were touring Australia in 1969, I was interviewed by a journalist for the major Melbourne daily. I had to suffer one of those yawning breakfast interviews which, although I was not at my brightest at 8.00 a.m., was really quite straightforward. Later that day, however, I met the same journalist again at a reception, and we began an off-the-cuff chat about superstitions.

I told him, purely as part of a conversation, that while I had been in Australia I had discovered I had a lucky bra, which had to be ready every day I thought I might have to bat. Many sports players are superstitious – some footballers will always put on one boot before another; golfers will only use a certain club on a certain tournament circuit – and I genuinely believed this one Berlei bra was lucky, because every time I wore it, I scored plenty of runs: what you would call loyal support, I suppose! We had a laugh about the stupidity of it all and I thought no more about the subject until I picked up the paper to read my interview the next day. Of our 'official' chat over breakfast, hardly a word could be found, but the headline over the article read: 'ENGLAND CAPTAIN RELIES ON LUCKY BRA'. I suppose the day I read the headline 'ENGLAND MEN'S CAPTAIN RELIES ON LUCKY STRING-VEST' I shall know we are equal in terms of press recognition!

15 Speaking

Coupling the name of Princess Anne with that of the *Daily Express* newspaper and giving them both my thanks may seem an odd way in which to open a chapter on my speaking exploits. It was, however, the Princess and the paper which gave this branch of my life a great boost.

The saga began in December 1971. I was recently back from my honeymoon when the *Express* invited me to their Sportsman of the Year Luncheon, staged in all the chandeliered splendour of London's Savoy Hotel. It was a memorable function, but I saw no reason to doubt that my part in it was all over as the liqueurs were served before the awards were made. What I didn't know was that my stepson Simon had been on a vote-collecting campaign around his school, Wrekin College in Shropshire, and had drummed up about 150 votes ... for me. I think he had bullied all the younger boys to fill in their voting for me – or else.

Like the Miss World contest, the *Express* awards are announced in reverse order, from tenth up to first. As the top ten Sportswomen of 1971 were announced, I sat very relaxed, tapping my brandy glass, but woke with a start from that soporific after-meal feeling when Sir Max Aitken announced that sixth place had gone to Rachael Heyhoe Flint.

It was such a complete and utter surprise that I wasn't initially sure what I was expected to do. I stumbled my way up to the microphone behind the top table with the thought running through my mind that many of the four hundred world-class sports stars in the room were probably puzzling and mumbling, 'Rachael who?' I decided that, if nothing else, I had better mutter a few words of self-introduction.

I obviously had no notes prepared for I had never expected

the need for speaking to arise. My delivery, the *Express* explained the following day, was slow and deliberate. To me, it was more like hiccup and miss. After briefly introducing myself, I managed to get a plug in for women's cricket, and in the search for a way to get myself off I used a line that I had many times employed when speaking at club functions.

'Those of you who go to see women's cricket', I began, 'will probably watch each girl going out to bat and wonder what they wear in the way of protection. Wonder no more. It's quite simple, really – we wear coconut shells.'

The place erupted, but, thrilled though I was by the reaction, I hardly dared to look down for I had suddenly remembered that the principal guest by my right elbow was Princess Anne. I was horror-struck that she might have thought my joke offended protocol and was not in particularly good taste. But I plucked up courage, bravely glanced to my right, and found to my enormous relief that the Princess was roaring with laughter. The photographers were quick to notice it too, and a picture of the moment appeared on the front page of the following day's *Express*. (It is reproduced in this book.)

Twelve months later, the inter-city train carrying me from Wolverhampton to the next *Daily Express* lunch had reached the outskirts of London when I began to wonder if Simon had been vote-hunting again. So, being slightly presumptious but chiefly cautious, I prepared a few anecdotes to relate, just in case there should be a repeat performance. There is nothing worse than being ill-prepared before making a speech. Few people are capable of speaking efficiently and entertainingly off the cuff, and I always feel safer with a speech outline – just a few notes and prompts, before I stand up and deliver, wherever it may be.

On this occasion, it was just as well I had played safe. I was named in fourth place, and despite setting off from my table towards the top table with every intention of collecting my award and saying nothing, I was detained by the microphone by the last thing I could have imagined – royal request.

The toastmaster for the event was Ivor Spencer, perhaps one of Britain's best-known in his job in recent years, and as I arrived to shake hands with Sir Max Aitken, Ivor was receiving a whispered message from Princess Anne, Sportswoman of the Year in 1971 and back at the luncheon again. She wanted me to speak.

In the book called *Pray Silence* which Ivor Spencer wrote later he named me as one of the best women speakers he has heard, together with Sheila Hancock, and explains that this was the only occasion when he had ever been given a 'royal command' to ask someone to speak.

Obviously I couldn't say no and rush off back to my seat. So I stood and spoke, updating the audience on my game and then expanding on the protection story. 'If over the last year any of you have been looking for the coconut shells, I'll give you a tip. You can always tell when a woman cricketer is wearing them, because when she goes out to bat it sounds like the Lone Ranger coming over the hill.'

The response was equal to the previous year's; ITV recorded the moment for 'World of Sport' and the *Express* captured another picture, featuring part of my head but much more of the Princess and Jackie Stewart laughing at the 'Lone Ranger'. The picture was entitled 'The Day the Princess laughed' and formed part of a folio which was to win the cameraman a Photographer of the Year award.

Just a month or so later, I was to hear more from Ivor Spencer. He phoned me one day in early 1973 to tell me that I had won the Guild of Professional Toastmasters' award as After-Dinner Speaker of the Year. I was the latest in a line of winners including such distinguished names as Lord Mancroft, Harold Wilson and Clement Freud, but for me the thrill of receiving the solid silver plaque and the accompanying honour was doubled by the fact that it was presented to me by the dear late Graham Hill.

Graham himself had been the 1972 winner, and in all my years in sport I could not wish to meet a more wonderful man.

He was touchingly kind to me at the presentation dinner in London's Dorchester Hotel; in fact, he was the same whenever we met. I, along with millions, was so sad when he was killed.

Being honoured by the toastmasters, who, after all, must have heard more rambling after-dinner speakers than anyone else, had its hidden disadvantages. Thereafter, whenever I was asked to speak at a function, however grand or humble the occasion might be, the patrons expected to find themselves rolling on the floor with laughter because of my award.

It happens everywhere, I suppose; once success has been achieved success is always expected. It's just like that with my speaker's award. But it makes it no easier for me to know that everyone expects the earth every time I stand to compete with the consumption of port and brandy and the billowing cigar smoke.

As my speaking engagements began to take me to more diverse occasions, I also realised that what was basically the same speech and series of anecdotes could be well received with a standing ovation one night and go down like a lead balloon the next. It made me realise that the greatest difficulty for any speaker – or any entertainer, for that matter – is to gauge what his audience will appreciate and adapt accordingly.

Nowadays I am often asked to stag dinners, and I always go along without ever being quite sure what I am expected to do. At one I particularly recall, one of the organisers proudly told me before the meal that 'Blaster Bates' had been their speaker the previous year and had entertained them all with a particularly blue brand of humour. I got the impression that he was hoping for something similar from me, but I had to disillusion him. I wasn't sure whether I had to do the dance of the Seven Cricket Pads!

Often I am expected to be a stand-up comedienne; and those who expect a string of crude barrack-room stories might as well not bother to come along – I wouldn't tell them even if I understood them all! No one could ever accuse me of being a prude, but downright vulgarity, particularly from a woman is just not necessary. It only loses respect and I undertake speaking engagements in the hope that I might gain respect.

Inevitably, stories have become attached to my name over the years. One in particular has caused me and my family no end of embarrassment. Perhaps because of my 'coconut shells' line, my name grew to be synonymous with stories about women cricketers' protection. But I must, right here and now, deny the myth that it was I who perpetrated the one about female cricketers wearing manhole covers.

The history of that tale in fact dates back to 1963, when Colin Cowdrey's eleven played against an England women's side at Chislehurst. Peter Parfitt and Peter Richardson, two England batsmen, were in Colin's side, and it was they who concocted the story, while chatting together in the slips.

I know it has been used at countless dinners with my name closely attached, but let me stress again, "Twas not me yer honour!' It was also very inaccurately attributed to me by a well-known women's magazine, which even had the audacity to put it in my quotes as having been related at the 'Princess Anne *Express* lunch' at the Savoy. That almost led to a writ of libel being served, for there was a rapid exchange of letters between my solicitor and the magazine.

The toastmasters' award brought me a good deal of publicity and approaches from professional speaking agencies. I have since worked for one, run by Cyril Fletcher and his wife, but with far less frequency since the arrival of Benjamin.

Marriage and motherhood have naturally added new demands to my life and I have made a deliberate move to cut down, almost cut out, evening speaking commitments. There are obvious domestic reasons why it is undesirable to travel all round the country, and family responsibilities are more important than self-glorification. Just as important in the decision, however, was my fear of letting anyone down at the last minute. I would far rather refuse a speaking invitation at the outset than tag the organisers along and withdraw at short notice – that is unforgivable.

My other speaking dislike is being asked to talk from the centre of a ballroom or hall. Psychologists would no doubt tell me that it is a sign of insecurity, but the fact remains that I feel more comfortable when I am speaking from the top table, with everyone else in front of me. I can never relax when I am addressing half the room and know that another half are studying my back view (not my best aspect!). Oddly, I am the same at parties, where I always prefer to stand on the edge of a room looking in, rather than standing surrounded in the centre.

The classic advice for after-dinner speakers is that they should talk for a minimum of five minutes and a maximum of ten minutes, unless specifically requested otherwise. That way, if you have any talent at all, you will leave the audience wanting more – which is the ideal time to sit down.

At one Variety Club function I attended in Leeds I was billed as the last of eight speakers. It had begun early on a Sunday evening, and the opening speaker got up just before eight o'clock. Believe it or not, it was almost three and a half hours later, at 11.15 p.m., that I finally had the chance to stand up and survey my audience – numb, tired and unreceptive. The seven speakers, an auction and several announcements before me had occupied far too much time. Apart from the fact that eight speakers seems too many anyway, it left me, as the tail-ender, with little hope of rousing the audience from their slumbers.

Since the days of Princess Anne and the *Daily Express* lunches, I have twice spoken in the presence of other members of the Royal Family. In Harrogate in 1975, I spoke at the Yorkshire County Cricket Club dinner which was attended by their patroness, the Duchess of Kent. It was a great thrill to meet such a charming person – who had the added attraction of loving cricket!

The other occasion, which drained my nerves more than

any other, came in November 1974 at London's Hilton Hotel. It was the Tenth Anniversary Ball of the Anglo-American Sporting Club – quite an awe-inspiring event in itself, but the reason I took fright was that I had looked at the menu on arrival and found that I was third speaker, trailing in behind David Frost and Prince Charles!

Since making speaking an integral part of my life, I have consciously collected anecdotes and jokes from every available source, through sport and every branch of the media in which I have worked. The effort is undoubtedly necessary. But,

as I said before, I owe more to Princess Anne, the *Daily Express* and 'World of Sport' than to anything I could have engineered myself.

Another demanding occasion which I remember well was when Margaret Thatcher received the England and Australian women's teams in her rooms at the House of Commons in our Jubilee summer. Speaking in front of such a very capable but charming woman was quite nerve-wracking – particularly in view of the fact that she had a 'backing' of several erudite Conservative MPs with her!

Earlier when I had met Mrs Thatcher at a sports book launching we had had a short chat and I had asked her if she had any interest in sport. She replied that at school she enjoyed hockey. I then with political innuendo said, 'I imagine you were a right-winger' – and her reply put me in my place nicely, 'No, actually I was centre-half!'

I was back at the *Express* lunch in 1973. This time, after my sixth and fourth placings of the previous two years, I wondered if I would get some sort of mention as it was the year that we England women had won the first cricket World Cup. What a thrill – I was runner-up to Ann Moore, and this time I had come prepared with a speech. How thwarted I would have felt if I hadn't got an 'onorable mention!

Only a fortnight earlier, I had learnt that I was pregnant. Apart from the telling of close relatives and friends, I had kept the news very quiet, with my lunch speech in mind. Up on the platform, I solemnly announced that I would be unable to play any women's cricket the following year, 'because I have just become a member of the MCC'. When the startled murmurs of 'really' and 'good heavens' had died down, I went on, 'In my case, this does not stand for the Marylebone Cricket Club but the Mothercare Club.' Pause. 'I suppose you might say that my husband has caught me in the slips, and next June I will be producing my first bouncer.'

The response was quite incredible. Dickie Davies, compering the lunch for 'World of Sport' nearly fell off the stage;

Henry Cooper came up and kissed me, and everyone was roaring their approval.

At the time, I believed that the 1973 gathering would be my swan-song as a *Daily Express* speaker. I went to the lunch again in 1974 but, of course, you don't win any awards for having a baby, and for the first time in four years I felt fully confident that I wouldn't have to say anything. Wrong again! The dinner and awards were through earlier than expected and Sir Max Aitken announced that as they'd had 'no chance to hear from Rachael this year, perhaps she'd like to say a few words now'. I didn't escape from the tradition until 1976 when the lunch overran. But I would never complain – it was all great fun and also a tremendous boost to my trumpet-blowing exercises!

Above: 32 'This was our finest hour' – speaking at Lord's after the first-ever women's match in August 1976. Giving RHF the cricketer's glance are Jonathan Fry, chairman of Unigate Foods and nephew of the great C. B. Fry; Jack Bailey, secretary of the MCC; Gubby Allen, MCC Committee; C. G. Paris, president of the MCC. *Below:* 33 All the 'B's – Benjamin, bats, barrow, bear, ball and Batwoman!

Above: 34 Driving for cover – RHF batting against Australia at Edgbaston, 1976. *Below:* 35 Not many fine legs in sight! RHF sweeping – the ball, not the wicket – against Australia at the Oval during a marathon eight-and-a-half-hour innings for her career best of 179, the world's second highest women's Test score

16 Extras

Although I am seemingly wedded to my cricket bat, hockey stick, journalism, broadcasting, and promotion work, I do, to many people's surprise, still retain a great interest in the sort of things which most other 'normal' women are interested in – namely, the everyday things of life like eating, drinking, fashion and relaxation. I have therefore tried to set down here a selection of my attempts at being as normal as most women are in their everyday life!

Cooking
Derrick would definitely agree, when I say that cooking and being domestic certainly are not my strongest achievements. Our kitchen has been littered with a trail of failures since the day we were married (e.g. cauliflower put in to cook with a couple of boiled eggs, or bacon that simply disintegrated into a pool of black spiralling oily smoke when I talked too long on the phone).

I am sure I would enjoy cooking if I had more time, but I can hardly become the galloping gourmet if the only galloping I do is from my little office here at home, along the hall to the kitchen at 13.05 in a frantic scramble to produce lunch for Derrick at 13.25.

I cheat a lot: we have a splendid freezer centre in the village where not only do they provide a wonderful range of goodies which can fool most people if you whip the foil off quickly enough, but the manager in there loves to talk cricket.

I hate being not good at anything – or not good at things that I ought to be good at, namely cooking. Often we are invited out to dinner parties with friends, and I am embarrassed when I am only able to return their kindness with an offer of crisps and twiglets!

Our marriage has been enriched with tales of my better 'Fanny Haddock' disasters in the kitchen. You need a pilot's licence to work all the dials on our double oven, and on one occasion I accidentally left a joint of beef and a joint of ham cooking all night. I had put the timer on for the oven to cease its labour at midnight but by sheer genius managed to turn the timer through to 9.00 a.m.! The dog woke us in the early hours of the morning baying like one of the Baskerville hounds at the scent of the cremation that was occurring in the oven. I ignored the barks.

In the morning I realised with horror what a stupid thing I had done. I gingerly opened the oven door to discover the joint of sirloin shrunk to about the size of a mean hamburger; the ham had obviously been pre-shrunk for it was a more recognisable size – but when we cut it, it shreaded into hundreds of strands and we had to eat it by the spoonful!

I have yet to bake a cake in six years of marriage – I daren't in case I'm not strong enough to lift it out of the oven! But one Saturday, after we had been married a few months, when it was raining and my hockey was cancelled, I thought I would be a real devil and make some scones to give Derrick a treat, at the same time relieving my boredom at being stuck indoors. They started off separately on the baking sheet, but when I peeped in through the glass inspection door of the oven they had merged into one great slab. They were heaved out from the oven rock-solid (I almost needed a block and tackle), sticking in the tray and resembling a minor range of hills. I nearly fractured my wrist trying to cut them.

In the evening, just for a 'little joke' Derrick brought them out when some friends came round for a drink. Ian Whyte insisted on taking one. 'You're not going to eat it, are you?' I asked in horror. 'No,' he assured me, 'I'll just keep it handy and then whenever I think my wife is a bad cook I will just look at this scone and think she isn't so bad after all!'

I think our dustbins must have ulcers by now, I have condemned so many Cordon Noire efforts to their insides.

I also have little time for housework or ironing – not that I am dedicated to either – but we thankfully have a marvellous 'daily feather', Mrs Pye, who organises my chaos for me and helps look after Benjamin when my hands are full.

Eating

I love small dinner parties and eating out occasionally at our favourite haunt, The Spinney in a Wolverhampton suburb. I far prefer this type of eating to the massive dinner-dance affairs – the food is always superior and the atmosphere is more peaceful. Perhaps it is a sign of old age, but nowadays after a dinner I hate having to battle with conversation against the blare of an amplified group or band who seem intent on perforating one's eardrums. I suppose the reason I enjoy eating out is that it is a relief from the disaster-area in the kitchen.

I do wish that nearer Christmastime, however, luncheon clubs and sports clubs would vary their menus slightly. I find that so many of them, understandably I suppose, go for the traditional turkey or chicken meal. But, if only a thought was spared for the guest. It so happened that one year, when I was really doing the old speaker's round, I had something like fifteen Christmas meals within twenty-four days – so much that I thought I would go broody if I had any more poultry!

My food tastes are simple (like me, again!), although I do love meat cooked in rich sauces – probably because I can't do it myself. I am very partial to trout or veal, but I also enjoy a good curry as well as Chinese food.

My ideal meal begins with mixed *hors d'oeuvres* or whitebait followed by steak au poivre – I love the crushed peppers which crunch on that steak, cooked rare. I don't have a sweet tooth at all: cream gateaux, profiteroles and the like fail to attract me in the slightest, so I pass straight from the main course to the cheese board – brie, camembert or stilton really turn me on.

Drinking

I love a drink, but by that don't think I am a fully paid-up member of Alcoholics Anonymous. I suppose it might be considered unladylike if I say I prefer lager to most other drinks. When we are on tour, (invariably in hot countries), lager is the top of the popularity poll for me. I particularly enjoy Castle Lager from South Africa, Swan from Perth in Australia and Red Stripe from the West Indies.

While we were in Jamaica we were taken round the Red Stripe brewery in Kingston where the ice-cold beer really tickled my taste buds. When I got back to England I wrote to thank Red Stripe for their kind hospitality and ask if I could get any of their beer in England. The Kingston brewery referred me to their London export offices; they in turn redirected me to a distributor in Birmingham who, incredibly, told me I could buy as much Red Stripe as I wanted from a tiny emporium in Penn Fields, Wolverhampton – a mile and a half from my home!

Good wine, daquiris and champagne also appeal to my taste and I'm a glutton for brandies after dinner – though I know they are bad for my blood pressure, and they also make me very argumentative!

Derrick is primarily a beer drinker, and when he plays golf every Saturday in the winter, he and his partners always continue living their Jack Nicklaus moments in our local, 'The Dog and Gun' and I enjoy joining them for a couple of lagers.

Smoking

I gave up smoking when I was seven years old because the Woodbines gave me a hacking cough! My little boyfriend Robin and I used to puff away until we were green in the nearby allotments to master this thing called smoking. We even smoked lengths of balsa wood which brother Nicholas used to use to make model aeroplanes – and I can tell you that really lifted the skin off the roof of your mouth. If I smoked secretly at home, I used to flick the ash in a hole in my eiderdown – how dangerous that was!

During my college career I smoked more than at any time, mainly because it was the 'thing to do' to look really 'grown up'. Daft really, but you don't like to be left out in a crowd. At the beginning of term I could afford to smoke king size cigarettes, but by the end, it was a case of Players Anchor – three-puffs-and-they-were-gone!

Strangely though I gave up smoking when I married Derrick; it should have been the other way round really! We managed to stop smoking by group therapy: a doctor friend of ours, Peter Barnes, really gave us a most frightening talk about the perils of the weed; then, within our 'crowd' at the squash club, we only smoked our own cigarettes and never offered them around. When you felt you really wanted to make the break, you left your own packet at home, or threw them away. Others were on pain of death to offer you one – and that was how I stopped. Now I hate the smell of stale smoke, and I loathe people to smoke in my car. If they ask if they may smoke I say 'Yes, but you must only inhale'!

Reading and relaxation

Influenced I suppose by the type of life I lead, I hardly have any time for real relaxation – in fact I find it very hard really to relax. I am an avid reader of newspapers but rarely can I ever settle into a full-length novel. I will read sports books and magazines, and when it comes to the time that I might be appearing on radio quiz shows such as 'Treble Chance', 'Forces Chance' or 'Games People Play', I spend any available free time learning fascinating but otherwise useless bits of information from *Pears Cyclopaedia* or various sports reference books.

Many evenings nowadays, once Benjamin has been 'nailed'

into his bed, I have to 'hibernate' in my little den (the butler's pantry converted, because we haven't got a butler!). There I answer letters, write various articles on my 'tripewriter', compose a few begging letters in my constant search for sports sponsorship, and generally organise my cricket fixtures. I have written two books in four years (this is my third), and that also takes up a lot of spare time.

I used to play a great deal of squash – I managed to play for the county a few years ago – but that was when Wolverhampton was the only women's club in the county and if you were in the club first team you were also in the county side!

I would love to have the time to play more golf: my handicap at the moment is long clubs and bad language. I have the weapons but I haven't really the time, but once I hang up my hockey and cricket shoes, I shall have far more time to devote to that sport – says I, hopefully!

Watching

Television does play quite a part in my life either for the acquisition of sporting knowledge or for satisfying my fascination for news. When I have been typing in my office in the evening, I will nip out to watch the BBC nine o'clock news, return to rattle off a few more paragraphs or letters, then finally emerge for the ITN 'News At Ten'.

There are very few TV programmes for which I would purposely give up my time. Those that do command my royal viewing – apart from the news – are all sports programmes, quizzes (especially 'Mastermind', when Derrick and I have a competition to see who can answer more than five questions!), 'The Magic Roundabout' and 'Paddington'.

I must say I enjoy Saturday night TV from 'Starsky and Hutch', through Jimmy Hill and his 'Scratch of the Day' to Parkinson.

Theatre rarely gets a look-in in my life, although if London were nearer I would love to see the best London shows. Plays with a message leave me cold – I like to go out to be entertained and amused, not to be set a mental exercise which invariably leaves you feeling thoroughly depressed when you have solved the mystery of living.

Cinema doesn't appeal much. The last time I went was during our West Indian tour, when some of the girls and I visited a drive-in cinema in Kingston, where 'Funny Girl', significantly, was the main film. Half-way through, I had to go to the loo, and when I returned, the girls had played a cruel trick and moved the car. In what resembles a giant car park of about five hundred vehicles, it isn't easy to spot one in the dark, and as I stumbled about, my silhouette kept appearing on the screen, much to the annoyance of other patrons. I only found my way back to them after remembering that I'd left a drinking tumbler on the roof. Finding the highest vantage point in the park, I scanned the area until I saw the car with tumbler still in place, standing up like a little smoke funnel.

Listening

I drive something like 15,000–20,000 miles a year, so I naturally have plenty of time to devote to listening, either to my tapes on the cassette player or to the radio, to get me through my journeys with the minimum of boredom.

My tastes are quite diverse and not too high-brow. On tape I have music ranging from Dvorak to Andy Williams, Beethoven to Frank Sinatra, as well as Nat King Cole, the Carpenters, the Seekers and Caribbean Reggae music. I find often that the more exciting the music the faster I drive, so I would never dare play 'In the Hall of the Mountain King', otherwise I might go into orbit as the crescendo is reached in the closing bars!

I have also been forced to develop a liking for two special tapes in the car, the stories of Beatrix Potter and Enid Blyton. They were bought for Benjamin, of course, and they really help to amuse him on long journeys – so I now know off by heart *The Tales of Pigling Bland, Jemima Puddleduck* and *Squirrel Nutkin* in stereo!

I listen to Radio 4 more than most channels, mainly in an effort to keep up with current affairs, and I enjoy the discussion programmes; I always switch for the Radio 2 sports desk bulletins and latch on to 'Sport on 2' on Saturday afternoons. Radio favourites of mine are 'Any Questions?', 'My Word', 'My Music' with the brilliance and wit of Frank Muir and Dennis Norden and 'Start the Week'.

Driving

It is very fortunate that I love driving, because of my very high annual mileage.

I have always chosen cars with a sporty image – they say the type of car you choose reveals your personality – and I have tended towards extrovert vehicles, once I could afford them. These have progressed from three red MG Midgets to a yellow Austin Healey Sprite, through to a Bond Equipe GT convertible, a Triumph Stag, and currently a Ford Capri Ghia 3 litre with a sunshine roof.

I confess that I enjoy speed – with safety – and I enjoy a challenge! It always amuses me when I get the better of a male driver because so many hate to be overtaken by a woman and they'll burst a gasket in an effort to overtake again. They do say that men and women drivers are as bad as one another – it's just that the women are less ashamed of it!

I think the most frightening experiences I have had on the road have been on the continent, especially in France, Italy and on the German *Autobahns*. I once drove over to Cologne (not across the channel – that I crossed by air ferry!) to cover a women's world hockey tournament for Reuter. I found the pace at which traffic hurtles along the *Autobahns* quite terrifying – far more nerve-racking than driving on British motorways.

I admit to being an aggressive and impatient driver; so much so that Benjamin has picked up some of my expressions. If we are ever stuck in a jam now, he will always shout from his perch in the back: 'Come on, stupid traffic!' or 'Hurry up Dickie Lightning!' or 'Mummy, what's that white car with the blue light behind us?'

A couple of minor endorsements have coloured my licence, but I managed to quash one charge by doing a personal 'Perry Mason' act in court. It happened in Wolverhampton when I had parked, perfectly legally, close to a corner, before popping into a shop. When I came out I found four policemen lifting my mini-van on to the pavement because a furniture van could not get round the corner without hitting me or the 'keep left' bollards. I was fairly unhappy about it to begin with, but when one of the officers then proceeded to book me for causing an obstruction, I was furious.

There seemed little point in arguing with him on the pavement, but when my summons arrived, I opted to appear in court, defending myself. I hadn't quite realised what I was letting myself in for, as I had to go into the dock and do the 'so help me God' bit, but I was at least given the chance to cross-examine the policemen concerned.

I asked only two questions. 'Was I legally parked?' Answer: 'Yes.' 'Had I overstayed the limit?' Answer: 'No.' I rested my case and the magistrates, deeming that there was 'an area of doubt', dismissed the charge. The next day I was driving past the same spot when I noticed workmen painting yellow lines exactly where I had been parked – justice will always triumph!

Fashion

I would be telling a lie if I said I thought I was fashionable, but I have always tried to take notice of the many changes in fashion in order that clothes I buy will suit the many differing functions I have to attend.

My thoughts on clothes have changed over the years. When I was a teacher, I tended to keep my 'best' for special occasions, and while at school lived in those inelegant, non-figure-flattering tracksuits. Then, as I moved into the field of journalism, which, I suppose, took me from the cloistered existence of a school a little more into the public eye, I found I had to smarten up a bit. Mind you, a newspaper office is hardly the place to wear your *haute couture*, off-white outfits (even if I could afford one!), especially working on the sports desk where you often had to wallow in upset cigarette ash and spilt cardboard mugs of machine coffee.

At one stage my mode of transport dictated what I should wear. As I have mentioned elsewhere, my first vehicle was a Vespa scooter and at that time the 'with-it' fashion (which was almost without it) was short pencil-slim skirts. The day I collected my scooter I discovered that this type of skirt just did not suit my mode of transport, for when I stopped at a junction I had great difficulty putting my feet down on the road without hitching up my skirt. Consequently, an exhibition of my footballer's thighs was once revealed to some workmen mending the road at a junction – and I think one roadman almost shot the pneumatic drill through his foot.

When I look back at photographs of the mini-skirted days, I shudder. I mean, if you look at the picture showing me with Mike Smith and Billy Wright you will see an ample demonstration of the truth of the theory that the mini-skirt was really no more than a pelmet. As one comedian said, a mini-skirt should be like a speech – long enough to cover the details and short enough to be interesting!

Nowadays I always seem to shop at the wrong end of the season, seeking winter outfits in January and summer things in July. I have two favourite 'mature' boutiques in Wolverhampton – Dorothy Rowley and Carousel – and in both the assistants always have a great smile on their faces when I appear, because they know I'm ready to set them a few problems.

My greatest difficulty is that my figure hasn't been arranged in the most proportionate way. I have the type of shape which so many sportswomen are blessed with – the small busted, larger-hipped version – so I can rarely step into any outfit which doesn't need altering. In the case of trousers, for example, I start hopefully with a size 14 – and find I can't even get them over my thighs without exploding the zip; then I move into a size 16 and the trouser-ends make me look as though I have elephantiasis; so they shorten the trousers inches and inches (such a waste of material) and I loose all the flare which was fashioned into them. To get a dress to fit is also difficult – often the hips will fit but the bust-line will need a couple of tennis balls to fill the darts and pleats.

I tend to buy outfits to suit specific occasions which are comfortable, simple, conventional and will not crease if you look at them. I tend to be fairly conservative in choice and for this reason my ensembles don't date too quickly. If I was daft enough to afford some *avant garde* creation, it would obviously be out of fashion within a year and would have to be given to the Wolverhampton Ladies' Cricket Club jumble sale – well, they do appreciate a bit of class, the devotees of jumble sales in Wolverhampton! At one such event years ago my mother gave an old fur coat which a frantic buyer snapped up for five shillings. My mother was horrified to hear the woman say that it would make a lovely rug for the kitchen floor!

During the day at home I'm invariably in trousers teamed with sweaters or shirts – not ravingly fashionable, but practical for sitting at my desk typing or scrambling around with Benjamin who, at just over four, is a cross between a Sherman tank and Action Man.

I enjoy dressing up for 'occasions'. Very often, if I'm travelling to London for something special, I will take my outfit in a British Airways portable 'wardrobe' and once the inter-city train passes Hemel Hempstead I change into a pumpkin in the loo. Not the easiest of tasks: putting on a pantie-girdle is pretty tricky in such a confined space and a lurch of the train can leave you upended with your head practically in the wash basin and an award of 5.9 for artistic impression!

Speaking at dinners demands a comfortable, non-fussy out-fit as far as I'm concerned: I don't want flapping boa feathers, frills or flounces to occupy more attention than the pearls of wisdom falling out of my shell-like lips.

As far as fashion on the field of play is concerned, many followers of women's cricket suggest that we should wear trousers rather than the short, white, divided skirt. My feelings on this are also divided – like the skirt – for although trousers are very much more accepted as fashion wear for women, to look really good in them you need slim hips and height. Many women cricketers just do not possess these qualities, and therefore for the bending, stretching and rapid movement while fielding, the skirts suit the job better. I wonder, though, whether trousers might be better for when we are batting, to do away with that unsightly gap between sock top and the knicker line when bending over the bat at the wicket. Both the Indian and West Indian girls wear trousers, and their slimmer players look super, so perhaps it might come for the English girls one day.

On sunny summer days, in the privacy of our garden, I always wear shorts and a suntop while I sit and type outside in the sunshine. I bring the phone out of the window on an extended lead (my outside line), and I think when callers hear the birds twittering in the background they must imagine I keep canaries!

I have a weekly pilgrimage to Nicholas the hairdressers up in Tettenhall village just for an hour of pure relaxation. Every four months or so I have a longer session there when I have highlight streaks added to my ordinary mid-brown hair. I've known Nicholas for almost twenty years, since he was an apprentice, and an hour at his salon, with no phone calls and plenty of laughs is very therapeutic.

Holidaying

I love the sun and all I ask for a real holiday is endless hours of sunbathing by a pool or on a beach. I am a real bore on vacation – I'm often berated because I have seen more swimming-pools round the world than ancient monuments. What I certainly never want from a holiday is a daily hike in search of crumbling ruins (ancient piles, as I call them), seeking out history.

Bermuda is one favourite spot, although I've only stayed there once. I love their whiter-than-white-roofed houses, clean and scrubbed-looking, their fabulous golf courses and their quiet way of life, which at first needs time to adjust to – an implicit 20 mph speed limit is adhered to. Eventually you settle into the slow, unworrying existence, and the return to England's more hectic pace is a real wrench.

The best holidays of our lives have been spent with Jack and Jean Hayward in their delightful colonial-style house on Grand Bahama Island. The setting is idyllic, with lawns fringed with palm trees, stretching down to the dazzling white beach and aquamarine-blue sea.

The pattern of each day is no less perfect. Waking at a leisurely hour to the sound of the sea crashing on the beach is the starter for the day. Then we progress from breakfast on the balcony in the sun to a morning of sunbathing and reading by the pool (one of the few chances I have to read!). Aperitif time comes next with subtly spiced Bloody Mary's as a prelude to lunch on the patio. Time then for a siesta and a walk up and down the beach to get the all-round tan, returning in time for a traditional English tea and fruit cake and a listen to the BBC World Service and sports news on short wave. Then it is cocktail hour with mouth-watering daquiris, followed by a change for dinner which is often eaten round an open fire, for it can get chilly in the evening. Then we sink into brandies, card games, quizzes, puzzles and conversation. Can't think how I can stand the strain of such a marvellous life!

17 Superstars

Taking part in a televised 'Superstars' competition was realising another ambition, because I always felt that women should have an equivalent competition to that of the men. I'd even tried to persuade ITV to do such a programme in 1974 – but no takers!

My chance came during 1976, when the BBC decided that the women should be given a try at their highly successful multi-sports marathon. I was called up along with seven other sporting females, and my first look at the opposition brought home the severity of the challenge.

Charlotte Brew, who took women into the Grand National, was the first name to catch my eye. The others followed in an impressive list: Anne Brightwell, the 800 metres gold medallist in the Tokyo Olympics; Divina Galica, ski champion turned Formula One motor-racing star; Gillian Gilks, first lady of world badminton; Donna Murray, Britain's blonde 400 metres sprinter; Karen Morse, European water-ski champion; and Denise Burton, the international cyclist.

Apart from the fact that I was giving away a good few years to all these girls, they were generally involved in sports which demanded a higher level of physical fitness than I had ever needed to achieve. Gillian Gilks, for example, does two or three hours' circuit training a day, plus a couple of hours badminton – all I do is rush from my typewriter to the kitchen to my car to the shops and chase Benjamin! It was a worrying thought, and it was that fear of looking a complete and utter fool which persuaded me to go into an intensive training programme for the first time in my life.

When Derrick and I returned from a swift winter break in the sun of Ibiza, only a fortnight was left before the contest. I went mad on every day of those two weeks, putting Benjamin to bed early each evening, then rushing out in heavy disguise as an athlete, to run either across the golf course near our house, or out round the roads. I borrowed a cycling machine and devised a circuit-training course round our house, involving the attic as well as the cellar steps! I even borrowed a bicycle, and went to the extent of using the Wolverhampton and Bilston Athletic Club's facilities for my training, much to the amusement of their 'real' athletes, such as Verona Elder and Rosemary Wright (formerly Stirling). A teacher friend, Lyn Jenkins, also helped me train in her school gymnasium, and she worked me till I dropped!

Before travelling down to St Ives, Cambridgeshire, I consulted a local naturopath and osteopath friend, both for exercises to get me moving more freely and for advice on what to eat to get the most instant energy. Under his directions, I arrived at the competition HQ armed with nuts, raisins, glucose and honey.

None of this managed to work the miracle I would have needed, however, and I finished seventh out of the eight! I decided youth was not on my side. Alone behind me in the ratings was Denise Burton, the little Yorkshire girl and daughter of an even more famous cyclist, Beryl. Poor Denise had great difficulty, and whenever commentators David Vine and Ron Pickering interviewed her on her chances in a particular event, she would say: 'I don't know about this one. All I do is ride my bike.'

Swimming was the opening event, but I chose to opt out because I always maintain that if we had been meant to swim well, we would have been given webbed feet and hands. I didn't fancy my chances, and anyway my water-wings had a slow puncture!

Next was another water sport, canoeing, which we had all spent most of the previous day practising. I just missed the final and finished fifth, but the highlight of the event was provided by the men, who were staging their own competition simultaneously for broadcast at another time. Shot-putter Geoff Capes was rammed by Welsh rugby star J. P. R. Williams, and made his feelings known so loudly that the retired folk sitting peacefully on the river bank looked as though they might fall in from the shock at hearing such profanities echoing across the peace and sanctity of the River Ouse.

In the basketball shooting competition, I finished joint third, but dropped to fourth after losing a sudden-death play-off against Karen Morse.

By now, I was becoming increasingly frustrated with my ineptitude against all these fit, young things. I determined to do something about it in the gymnastics test.

This was in fact more like a combat course, which included vaulting, rope-swinging, scaling wall bars, squat thrusts, balancing on a beam, somersaults, hurdling and a final sprint for the tape. Hurling myself at every obstacle like an inelegant Tarzan-cum-Action Man, I even surprised myself by finishing second to the elegant winner, Donna Murray. If I achieved nothing else, I thought, this has saved my pride.

The second morning of the competition began with the hockey event, in which I was established as favourite. Although I have played most of my top-level hockey in goal, there have been occasions when I've been used in outfield positions, and the rest of the girls seemed to think that I should have been barred from this event. When it was all over, I wished I had been!

Each girl had to dribble through sticks set up in slalom fashion, before shooting against a goalkeeper from anything beyond a five yards line. We had three attempts each and the results were worked out first by the number of goals scored, then, to split ties, on a time basis. Even I imagined that I ought to do well in this. Instead, I failed to score a single goal and finished way down the order. The goalkeeper stuck out a leg to deflect my first shot, then I topped the second and missed with the third – all very embarrassing – and how were the mighty fallen!

The cycling event was run off in heats of two on a match-race basis, but as seven girls had entered, one had to race alone against the clock. I was drawn for the solitary ride, and despite loud vocal support from American Air Force men who came from a nearby base, I failed to qualify for the final – perhaps I was carrying too much excess baggage!

Finally, I chose to give the 100 metres a miss and compete in the 400 metres, where I calculated I would have more chance of struggling through and keeping pace with the pack. Six girls were in the race, and as I was in the outside lane, I led dramatically for the first 20 yards. A steady, and remarkably loud and ominous thumping of little feet behind me announced that I was being caught, not just by one or two, but by everybody: I was left trailing in a pretty poor sixth place. I later heard Ron Pickering's commentary in which he expressed the view that some of us would experience an oxygen debt after 300 yards. I had news for him – I suffered it after 50 yards!

Rounding the final bend into the straight, all that I could see was a row of white bottoms crossing the finishing line and a few arms flung up to the sky. My legs just wouldn't carry me any farther at a run, so I decided to cover my embarrassment with a slow-motion imitation of the Bionic Woman, which at least entertained the crowd. As I crossed the finishing line, seemingly minutes after the others had finished, Maurice Simmonds, the sales and distribution director of Schweppes, the event sponsors, caught my arm and led me into the hospitality tent. He explained that I looked very pale and he thought I needed a brandy to revive me. How right he was – I think I almost needed the kiss of life as well!

I certainly didn't set Superstars alight, but I was extremely happy to have been invited to compete in such exalted company. Perhaps in the future I can put in some more training and do a little better in a veterans' 'Superstars'!

Another of the daft things I let myself in for was a charity motor-racing event at Brands Hatch. It was run in March of

1976 on Race of Champions Day, with the proceeds going to the SPARKS charity. Sixteen sportsmen were invited to compete in the race – or, to be more precise, fifteen sportsmen and me! I found myself up against such greats as David Hemery, Henry Cooper, Colin Cowdrey, Fred Titmus, David Duckham, Chay Blyth and Reg Harris, and I must say I found it all very easy during our practice session a week before the race. Driving round Brands Hatch in a speedy Cortina 3 Litre GT was my idea of fun. When race day itself arrived, though, it was all very different.

As the only lady involved, I was given the privilege of pole position, which terrified me from the start. Sitting on the grid at the front of the pack with thousands and thousands of spectators packed in the stand just made my legs turn to jelly. Brother Nicholas came to support (Derrick was too scared!), but when I tried to speak to him from my car, my tongue had stuck to the roof of my dry, nervous mouth!

The event was run on the lines of a serious top-class race, and as I sat revving up my car, strapped in complete with helmet, overalls and all, I turned to the driver of the other car at the front of the grid, hoping for a bit of comfort – just a smile would help! But I'd chosen the wrong man. Next to me was Chay Blyth, and when you've sailed single-handed round the world, I suppose you have a competitive streak that will not even relax for a charity event like this. He gave me a steely, grudging smile then turned to stare ahead again.

My initial feeling when the flag came down was one of relief that I shot forward instead of reversing into the car behind. I was race leader for at least 50 yards, and almost got first into the opening bend but then all hell let loose.

We had been told to keep to the right of the track if we were being overtaken, but as I tried to pull over that way, I saw in the mirror that a car was already streaking alongside. I went to the left and found the same thing, so, resigned to my fate, I sat in the middle of the track and let the others fight it out among themselves.

Two men didn't complete the course and I finished four-teenth – yes, last of the finishers. But my embarrassment at being the back marker became even more obvious when the race was all over. After completing the final lap, I missed the entrance into the pits, and found myself forced to do another circuit, behind Chay Blyth who had won the race and was on his lap of honour. Most of the crowd probably thought I was the runner-up and I joined in the misunderstanding by regally waving to acknowledge the cheers.

The worst was still to come, for I somehow managed to miss that darned entrance yet again, and this time I completed a lap of dishonour behind the ambulance and breakdown truck which were clearing the track for the next race.

My initiation into the world of motor-racing told me one thing at least – that I certainly haven't got the courage to follow Divina Galica, who started her career in the sport in a similar race.

If motor sport did not agree with me, soccer certainly did on the memorable night that I ran out to a 20,000 crowd at Molineux to keep goal for an ATV team in a benefit match for Wolves' captain Mike Bailey.

Standing under floodlights in those huge, imposing goals where my hero Bert Williams had played was an unforgettable experience for me. And I surprised a few people by at least showing that I could kick a football – and by putting up my umbrella when it rained! How I wish that such crowds would turn up in England and watch our Test cricket!

I must say I have loved my 'superstars' moments – albeit 'superflop' appearances as far as I'm concerned. I love mixing with the greats in sport and am amazed that playing two relatively minor sports should have enabled me to meet such super sportsmen and sportswomen.

18 Heroes

A few years ago, I was asked to name my favourite six male cricketers and explain my reasons. In no particular order, they were Dennis Lillee, Colin Cowdrey, Garry Sobers, Ray Illingworth, Basil D'Oliveira and Rodney Marsh. I have since had to make a substitute for the last named, as his play and attitudes on the field, plus his becoming a Packer defector, have changed my opinion of him. The other five remain high on my list of most respected players, and by adding another seven names here, I can compile the World XI, plus one, that I would most like to see in the field.

Choosing a world team is a popular pastime among cricket players and followers of all ages and nationalities – though no one's team can claim the projection achieved by Kerry Packer's – and the general criterion is playing ability alone. I have tried to be a little different, and select not just on skill but also on temperament, loyalty and personality, so that the majority of my choices are inevitably men I have met and admired.

My team sheet is headed by the name of Colin Cowdrey, who will always remain one of my greatest heroes. Again, my respect for Cowdrey does not stem just from his undoubted class as a batsman, but from his attitude, manners and general behaviour. He is the epitome of the English gentleman cricketer.

Cowdrey's arrival at the crease has frequently done more to settle a shaky team than any barrel of tranquillizers could have achieved. He bats as he lives – undemonstratively, but with a delightful hint of grace about every movement he makes. The drive has always been thought of as his finest stroke, and I think it is made still more attractive by his high, full follow-through along the line of the shot.

Colin is a man of quiet charm and complete politeness, yet one of his greatest qualities is bravery. It was never better illustrated than in England's home series against the West Indies in 1963, when he faced the fury of Wes Hall and Charlie Griffith with a calm composure that could have lulled one to believe they were bowling with a tennis ball. To his cost, Colin was made painfully aware that the ball was considerably harder than the tennis variety when a short one from Hall broke his forearm. But, summoning the sort of courage that one very rarely sees, he returned with his arm in plaster during the final over, thankfully not having to face a ball as England hung on for a draw.

His bravery was illustrated again in 1975 when, despite being at the stage of his career where he could have been excused for craving the quiet life, he answered the calls of an MCC team ravaged by injuries and flew to Australia. There, with no more than a few days of nets, he came into the Test side on the world's quickest wicket at Perth, and confronted the hostility of Dennis Lillee and Jeff Thomson as if he was twenty-five again. I loved Tony Lewis's description of Colin as he went out to bat, padded up to the eyebrows: he likened him to an amiable Womble.

In the field, his comfortable girth belies his sharp reactions, and for many years he pocketed half-chances at slip for Kent and England with amazing aplomb, often baffling many thousands of others by taking the catch, pocketing the ball and pretending not to know where it had gone to.

Cowdrey has played more Test matches than anyone in the game's history – well over a hundred – which is in direct contrast to the man I would choose to open the batting with him.

Barry Richards has suffered as much as anyone through South Africa's sporting exile. It is impossible to say what he might have achieved had he been permitted more than his paltry four Tests, but I have little doubt that he would have established himself among the greatest batsmen of all time.

Inevitably, he has eventually suffered through shortage of incentives, but when the occasion is right and his adrenalin is flowing there are few players in the world I would prefer to watch. Richards' range and timing of strokes when at his best can be absolutely captivating, and his apparent disregard for anything the bowlers can deliver often gives his batting a deceptively casual appearance. If he is in a driving mood, little can stop him and he can often be seen destroying the most blatant leg-side bowling with pure improvisation, stepping two feet outside leg stump to stroke the ball through the covers. Only a player of his ability would even attempt it.

My next batsman, and a very dear friend is Basil d'Oliveira. A charming, quietly-spoken South African, Basil is loved by cricket's masses not only for all-round ability but also for his diplomacy. A man of lesser principles would have sold his soul to the popular press several times over when he was banned by South Africa from touring their country with England in the late 1960s. It was a heartbreaking episode for him, which shattered his ambitions of a lifetime. But instead of taking the low way out and picking up a great deal of money for 'telling all', Basil held his head high and kept his feelings private.

Basil's batting has swung many matches when an innings of power and command has been called for, and even now, well into his forties, his county, Worcestershire, have spent months pleading with him to delay his retirement.

My favourite story of D'Oliveira is a personal one. I played in a men's XI – the Lye CC President's XI – at their small ground near Stourbridge to mark the opening of Lye's new pavilion. The men batted first and piled up the runs, with Basil depositing the ball for countless fours and sixes. He had scored 98 when I was rashly asked to bowl – a rare enough event in itself. My first ball was a medium-paced long-hop which Basil politely patted back to me. There was no greater venom in my next ball, but Basil stepped down the wicket, played all round the ball with conviction, and was bowled. He had fooled the crowd who thought I had genuinely dismissed him – but how many others could have brought themselves to do that when two short of 100? I mean, a century is a century, whatever standard the match may have been. As Dolly walked back past the square-leg umpire to the pavilion he commented that he'd never hit a woman in his life and he wasn't going to hit Rachael!

Basil's deceptive swing bowling off a jog-trot approach has broken many a partnership in Test and county cricket, but looking down the names in my side I think his opportunities with the ball may be few!

My number four batsman is the West Indies' Clive Lloyd, as breathtaking a striker of a cricket ball as I have ever seen. Lloyd is capable of taking any attack apart and has frequently done so. I suppose if his batting has a fault it is the one which afflicts almost every player to come from the Caribbean – that of being slightly impatient. At times when the West Indians are batting, it would seem that defensive shots had never been invented.

I shall never forget seeing him bat for Lancashire against Surrey in an early round of the Gillette Cup in 1977. Severely hampered by a leg injury which was to keep him out for most of the summer, he still turned the match with an amazing innings. On a leg and a half, he repeatedly smashed the ball out of the ground at Old Trafford, so what he might have been like on two good legs, heaven knows.

Although he now generally fields close to the wicket, Lloyd will also long be remembered for his speed and agility in the cover area. He moved rather like a panther across the grass, and threw with speed and impeccable accuracy. Watching him field reminds me of a human daddy longlegs – a tremendous character.

Following Lloyd in my batting order is another West Indian, the greatest cricketer that they or any other country has ever produced. Garry Sobers holds the distinction of being a genuine three-in-one player, whose ability could change the course of a match in so many ways. In fact, it is an understatement to say that Sobers has three qualities, because his bowling alone has that many. In his Test cricket days he could open the attack, loping in, arms flopping by his side, before delivering in classical style and with deceptive speed; then, when the need arose, he could turn to spin, bowling either orthodox slow left-arm or the tricky stuff out of the back of his hand. His fielding was versatile and faultless, and I remember seeing him pick up some seemingly impossible close catches, through a mixture of instinct and anticipation. But it was his batting which really caused most excitement. He used to glide out to the wicket as if on roller skates and bat with a relaxed look, almost casual in its confidence. While he was there and in full flow, the best any fielder could usually do was to take refuge somewhere quiet. Sobers' adventurous instincts often lead to his own downfall. But any man who can hit six sixes in one over is a man for me!

Mike Procter falls into the same category as Barry Richards. His Test career was cruelly cut short by the intervention of politics in sport, and he has since had to content himself with provincial cricket in South Africa and an inspiring role in the renaissance of Gloucestershire here in England. Had he been allowed to further an international career that was just beginning to flourish in 1970, Procter would probably have succeeded Sobers as the undisputed all-round king of world cricket, as he has very similar skills.

Procter is a mighty batsman, whom I have seen hit sixes with about as much effort as striking a match. Perhaps he has not scored as many runs as he might, however, due to the inevitable strain placed on his physique by his extraordinary bowling action. There are few more exciting sights in cricket than Procter hurtling in off that enormous run. When he gets to the crease, he appears to deliver off the wrong foot, and with an open-chested action that makes orthodoxy seem ridiculous. How he doesn't split his trousers every time he bowls, I will never know. Perhaps he uses specially strengthened stitching?

Godfrey Evans is my team's wicketkeeper. No disrespect to Godfrey, but had I had to choose a more current keeper, I would have plumped for Rodney Marsh or Alan Knott: they, however, have showed their disloyalty to their countries by defecting to Packer so I will stick by the true blue 'Godders'.

I only saw him play in the latter stages of his first-class career, but I was always very impressed by his spectacular agility, his delightful perky personality and his devil-may-care batting. In the past few years I have played on the same side and against 'Godders' in various charity matches and he still has amazing reaction for someone in his fifties. In one such 'mixed' six-a-side at the Oval, Godfrey was standing up to the wicket to the bowling of Graham Roope, the England and Surrey all-rounder, whose pace is fairly sharp, and he completed a most superb leg-side stumping that even a twenty-five-year-old would have been proud of.

Cricket has not always treated Ray Illingworth kindly. His service to the game has been tremendous, and his captaincy of England brought the success that we had been craving for years. Yet he was axed in 1973 in favour of Mike Denness.

It was an odd dismissal, to say the least, but Ray accepted it silently, refusing to be drawn into a slanging match despite the bitter disappointment he must have been feeling. I respect him for that.

Illingworth was never the gay cavalier with the flamboyance of several recent international captains. He was hard, though, and his authority on the tactics and strategies of the game could never be questioned.

His greatest achievement was winning the Ashes on the 1970–1 tour when more unrest was stirring behind the scenes than any outsider could have realised. He then retained the Ashes at home in 1972. A year later, he was gone.

Since then, Illingworth has been working his Yorkshire magic on his adopted Leicestershire, combining trenchant batting and marvellously skilful off-spin bowling with un-matched leadership. Soon he will go home to coach at Yorkshire, and I'm sure that will come as easily to him and bring as much success as everything else in the game.

I couldn't leave Dennis Lillee out of my world side. To me, he is an awe-inspiring bowler, whose talent is matched only by his courage in coming back from an injury that would have finished many players.

Lillee takes off from near the boundary boards and launches himself towards batsmen like a warrior charging into battle. His long hair flaps, and his eyes peer intently from his impressively set face. The delivery itself is such an explosion of power and energy that I often wonder why his follow-through never lands him in the batsman's lap. At the tender age of twenty-two he was torturing English batsman, inducing shots that they had no intention of playing and no hope of avoiding. He is still among the world's powers as I write this, and he could have the new ball every time in my side.

There are many stories about Lillee's belligerence, even his abuse of batsmen. But the thing I have always noticed about him is that at the end of a successful over, he will slink modestly off to the relative quiet of the deep outfield, as if apologising for his own skill.

Although I never knew him when he was at his best, I must have Fred Trueman in my side. He is perhaps the English Lillee, although it would be fairer in terms of chronology to say that Lillee is Australia's answer to Trueman. He raced in with the same venom in his eyes, a similar mop of dark hair flopping around his face. The delivery was copy-book, and although he may never have been as fast as Lillee at his quickest, he certainly did far more with the ball.

Fred was a great character while playing, and remains so now that he has an observing role as commentator and writer on the game. It would answer a dream of mine to have Lillee and Trueman opening the bowling together – and I fancy it would bring the nightmares of a thousand and one batsmen to reality!

I complete my twelve with two men best known for spin

bowling – Australia's Richie Benaud and the West Indies' Lance Gibbs.

Benaud, of course, is still a prominent figure in the game as a television commentator and now a co-ordinator for the Kerry Packer troupe. But while playing, he was not only one of the finest leg-break bowlers of all time, but a valuable middle-order batsman and an inspiring, handsome captain. It occurs to me that I have selected so many natural leaders that it would be an impossible task to pick a captain for my World XI.

Like most people, my abiding memory, almost my only memory of Gibbs is of watching him rush through an over in about sixty seconds. His short, prancing approach, the teasing delivery of immaculate length and wicked turn, the defensive stroke and he was back at his mark and wheeling to bowl again. The whole operation was over so quickly, yet he frustrated more batsman than any other bowler I have seen. I once batted against him in a benefit match on a poor-quality club pitch, and I have never seen a ball turn so sharply; I played forward to one ball on the off-stump which bit, turned and lifted and the keeper took the delivery down the leg side. It made my eyes pop out like chapel hat-pegs!

Gibbs also passed Fred Trueman's record of 307 Test wickets, although Fred will tell you he bowled many more overs than he was allowed to. I'd like them in the same side.

That completes my line-up; five Englishmen, two Australians, three West Indians and two South Africans. It's all a fantasy of course – but why shouldn't I have my moment of power as a selector!

19 Future

When I first heard the news on the BBC World Service 'Sports Round-up' that the England women had lost the World Cup in India while I was sitting at home on a cold January day in 1978, I was initially numbed and sad, and I wished I could have helped my friends against Australia. However, in cricket there is never any guarantee that any individual can work a miracle or alter the end result of a match.

It seemed, however, the final irony in a year of losses by English women's cricket, most if not all of which could quite simply have been avoided. Our government grant was reduced, and consequently our paid National Development Officer was lost, as we could not prove sufficient progress to justify her. Our previous sponsors, St Ivel and Unigate, were lost to the game. Our patron and greatest benefactor, Jack Hayward, resigned after my sacking. Now the World Cup was lost. Could anything else have gone wrong?

It astounded me, therefore, that the Women's Cricket Association's annual meeting at Lord's in January was conducted with an apparently bland lack of concern by the officers. They didn't seem to realise just how far backwards the game might go, or indeed had gone, nor how difficult it would be to regain that ground. In fact, they seemed enthusiastic only about directing veiled and barbed comments at me, all of which were quite pathetic. For example, there were comments in the chairman's report to the effect that she had heard that some players were playing for money – but when pressed from the floor for details, she could not give any; and that there ought to be a code of conduct for players as to how to conduct themselves on radio and television and in the press.

Jack Hayward had timed his letter of resignation to arrive on the day of the meeting. On the question of sponsorship the immediate past chairman, Miss Swinburne, spoke out with another anti-Flint remark, saying that she had just done her homework and that the association hadn't really needed a sponsor for 1976 after all – and what good were champagne breakfasts at Heathrow, to welcome the Australians, and receptions at the Savoy? What a pity, I thought, that she didn't do such homework in 1974, so that I would have been saved two years' hard work trying to find a sponsor. During those two years of searching I was constantly phoned by Miss Swinburne: 'Have you got a sponsor yet? We shall have to call the tour off if we don't get one,' etc.

I quote Jack's letter of resignation below, and I think his words are as apt as any ever written about my unhappy year:

I feel strongly that the present committee and last year's selectors did great damage to the image of women's cricket in general, which over the past few years so many of us have worked so hard to promote.

Everyone I have spoken to felt that the way Rachael was dismissed was very badly done, to put it mildly. I would like to have had yours and the committee's opinions also, but when I asked you at Lord's why you had not made a statement of explanation, you replied that 'It might establish a precedent'!

I can only gather from this remark that last summer's methods are going to be employed with future England captains!

I think the silence of you and your committee has been very damaging, not only to Rachael personally but to women's cricket as a whole and its public relations which was riding so high before last summer.

I am, of course, very fond of Rachael, who first brought me into women's cricket, which I do not regret for a moment as it has been great fun up to the past eight months.

I sincerely believe that the selectors have erred over the past few years in not properly grooming a successor for Rachael, who, perhaps, should have given up the captaincy a year or two ago.

I think I can sum up my feelings, and those of just about everyone I have talked to throughout the world on this subject – and it has reverberated throughout the world – by saying that 'It was not her going that was so distressing, but the manner of her going.'

The letter was sent to Rosemary Goodchild, who may, for all I know, treat Jack's departure with about as much regret as she treated mine. But the chairman's reply admitted that the association had been wrong in the way affairs were handled and that some professional guidance in public relations would have been an advantage! She then added that she considered that 'Rachael herself' could have 'made some more positive moves' . . . like resign before the balloon blew up, I suppose, and clear the way for the WCA without the resultant furore!

The whole stupidity of the situation became even more apparent at an early 1978 WCA executive meeting. A draft document was circulated to the representatives at the meeting relating to WCA public relations. The specific proposals included the announcement of the appointment of a PR company and new initiative being taken by the WCA; starting a hunt for sponsorship with press announcement and follow up; the maintenance of a sustained flow of press news and releases and features about development, events, etc, etc. The staggering revelation was that the WCA was prepared to spend £5,000, in this so-called initiative, to a PR company, for a year's work – the type of work which I and others had been doing, for love, for ten years!

At least it's nice to know how much one's effort is worth in terms of hard cash. Just think, ten years' work at £5,000 per annum equals £50,000 – that would certainly have made my piggy-bank bulge!

Women's cricket undoubtedly faces a stern test in the next few years. The West Indies are due in England in 1979, but during the first half of 1978, there was no indication of any forthcoming sponsorship. Until the WCA finally accept the advent of commercialism in sport, they cannot hope to survive at any credible or creditable level. They cannot go on supporting a sport with jumble sales and bazaars.

A punishing levy is still inflicted on all club players, and especially on those good enough to win a place on a tour. It is a farcical situation and players will soon make it known rather more forcibly that they don't want to spend their savings supporting an inefficient administration which gives them so little in return.

I will continue to channel efforts into raising money for women's sport, and, obviously, for cricket – but I stress that, for the time being, any fruits of my labours will go to the game as a whole and not the WCA. It is a pity, but I will no longer give money to people who feel they neither trust nor need me. If the personnel of the WCA officers alters, then my mind may be changed. But for now, the lack of trust is mutual and I don't intend to waste my time. If they don't like me as I am – well, I'm sorry I cannot change now: I've been the same now for too many years to alter my whole character!

Deep down, I know I now want to spend more time devoting myself to being a good wife and mother. However hard I may have tried in the past, I know I have been neglectful of both Derrick and Benjamin and the family at certain times.

Derrick, whose proudest moment came when Jean Rook in the *Daily Express* described him as a 'six-foot Greek Godlike creature', has been wonderfully understanding throughout and I couldn't have asked for greater support and kindness.

All that is not to say that I shall be giving up the playing side of either cricket or hockey. Far from it: I still feel I have a little to offer to both games, and the main thing is that I still enjoy playing sport. I can still take my own international

side around the world, and although we won't be England
and we won't quite have the patriotic flavour of Test cricket,
it will still be great fun – I shall see to that! And I can still
captain other England teams, as I discovered in February 1978
when my BBC Radio 2 quiz team on 'Treble Chance' won
through to the final – so there will always be some compensations for me round the corner.

Even as I write this book there has been an upheaval in the
make-up of the 1978 England women's selection committee.
Audrey Winterbottom, the all-powerful chairman of the committee who knocked me off my perch, chose not to stand for
re-election, although she had only held the office for a year.
Neither did two others of that committee, Kay Green
and Carole Evans, gain re-nomination. So who knows, the
door might not be finally closed. Only time will tell – but
of course, in that time I am not getting any younger. However,
I still console myself with the thought that Brian Close was
recalled to England aged forty-four; Jack Hobbs was playing
when he was forty-eight; and England needed Wilfred Rhodes
when he was fifty-two – so I still have some little hope.

With a name like mine there cannot surely be any more
Rachael discrimination; with a name like Flint I must be
hardened to any further downfalls and disappointments; and
with a name like Heyhoe it's being so cheerful that keeps me
going!

During the winter of 1977–78 I managed to obtain commercial backing from British Airways to run a British Airways
International Women's XI which would travel the country
(by car!) playing various men's teams. The press, of course,
likened me to Kerry Packer – the *Daily Express* headline read
'Now it's Rachael's Flying Circus' – but I made sure that
none of my fixtures disturbed established women's cricket
fixtures, that I didn't poach players and that our amateur
status was not infringed. The whole irony was that what I
had negotiated for my own XI could so easily have been for
the benefit of the WCA.